GET MONEY:
Self-Educate, Get Rich & Enjoy Life
Volume 1

The Cell Block Presents TCB University

The Cell Block Presents TCB University

FREEBIRD
PUBLISHERS

Freebird Publishers
Box 541, North Dighton, MA 02764
info@FreebirdPublishers.com
www.FreebirdPublishers.com

Toll-Free: 888-712-1987
Phone/Text: 774-406-8682

Copyright © 2017 GET MONEY:
Self-Educate, Get Rich & Enjoy Life
Vol. 1 By The Cell Block

All rights reserved. No part of this book may be reproduced in any form or by any means without the prior written consent of the Publisher, except in brief quotes used in reviews.

All Freebird Publishers titles, imprints and distributed lines are available at special quantity discounts for bulk purchases for sales promotions, premiums, fundraising educational or institutional use.

ISBN-13: 978-1979760553
ISBN: 1979760551

Printed in the United States of America

Disclaimer: While the publisher strives to make the information in this book timely and accurate as possible, the publisher makes no claims, promises, or guarantees about the accuracy, completeness, or adequacy of the contents of this book, and expressly disclaims liability for errors and omissions in the contents of this book. References in this book to any specific organization, law, party, process, or service, or the use of any trade, firm or corporation name is for the information and convenience of the public, and does not constitute endorsement, recommendation, or favoring by the publisher.

The Cell Block Presents TCB University

GET MONEY: Self-Educate, Get Rich & Enjoy Life, Vol. 1

Table of Contents

Part One: Get Money 9
   5 Core Steps to Starting Your Own Business…Even from A Prison Cell!...... 10
   5 Common Launch Errors You MUST Avoid! 11
   6 Tips to Rev Up Your Company This Year 12
   You Must Read This to Improve Your Business Success! 13
   How to Legally Protect Your Assets Once and For All!! 16
   Best Advice from 15 Self-Made Millionaires! 19
   The 6 Entrepreneurial Profiles! 21
   BO$$ Status: A Guide to Entrepreneurial Leadership! 23
   BO$$ Status: How to Build Your Team! 7 Keys to Team Development and Success! 24
   Bo$$ Status: How to Encourage Your Team! 26
   BO$$ Status: How to Be a Better Boss 29
   BO$$ Status: 3 Easy Step to Better Leadership! 31
   BO$$ Status: Focus on The Vision! 33
   How One Guy Made $20 Million In Under A Year... and YOU Can, TOO! .. 35
   How A TEEN Averages $2,800 In Monthly Profits! 38
   How to Make Money Doing Internet Info Searches for Inmates! 39
   How to Get Rich Selling Non-Nude Photos! 40
   How to Start an Independent Record Label in 9 Steps! 42
   Seven Secrets of Book Selling Success! 47
   How to Get Rich Publishing Material You Get FREE! 54
   How to Sell Your Own Subscription Newsletter for HUGE Profits! 56
   How to Get Rich Selling Information! 60

The Cell Block Presents TCB University

Get Rich Selling Real Estate (That You Don't Own!) 69
How a Teen Made Over $80,000! 72
10 Easy Ways to Build Your Social Media Following! 73
How to Find Your Audience on Social Media 74
How to Build a Facebook Page for Your Small Business 76
Twitter Tips for Your Business 77
12 Ways to Increase Sales With Social Media 78
Advanced Social Media Tips and Tricks! 79
Successful Promotional Letters & Marketing! 88
How to Maximize Marketing Dollars! 93
Change How You Think About Marketing: Go Inbound! 95
The 7 Steps of Effective Product Development 96
How One Company Turned Their Mission Statement into Big Bucks! 99
Your Brand is YOUR Story! 102
Part Two: Mailbox Money 105
How to Get the Most from Your Reports! 106
How to Make $1,000 Profit with A 1,000 Name Mailing List! 109
How to Get Free Mailing Lists, Stamps & Envelopes! 111
Customer Service Tips for Mail Order! 112
The Big Money Secrets to Selling Books by Mail!! 113
How to Start a Mail-Order Business on A Shoestring! 116
How to Get Orders in Your Mailbox 365 Days A Year! 117
Ad Designing Tips! 118
Avoiding Mail Order Mistakes! 119

How to Publish Your Own Ad Sheet for Big, BIG Profits!	120
Part Three: Surviving Prison	123
Paroling from Prison (my 2 cents)	124
Mental Health: The Secrets	128
Surviving the Hole: The Secrets	132

The Cell Block Presents TCB University

Part One: Get Money

5 Core Steps to Starting Your Own Business...Even from A Prison Cell!

START IT

Business startup isn't rocket science; it's not as complicated or scary as people think. Once you have a great idea, product or service in mind, it's a step-by-step common-sense process. Here's step one: Figure out what you want to do and do it.

PLAN IT

If you build it, will they buy it? Determining whether there really is a market for your product or service is fundamental. Consider market research an investment in your future product or service. Make the necessary adjustments now that will save you money in the long run.

FUND IT!
Figure out where the money will come from. The best place to begin is by looking in the mirror. Self-financing is the number-one source of income for startup -- and it creates faith in your company when you need more cash. Get the expert advice on how to approach bankers, investors, or crowdfund.

MARKET IT!

It's essential that you spread the word about your company/product/service. You can create a brand identity and develop a marketing campaign that works -without spending a fortune. However, an investment of your time is required.

PROFIT FROM IT!

Make sure you're in love with the profit, not the product. Many people get emotional about their business, which clouds their judgment. Keeping score with basic bookkeeping and financial statements will help you effectively manage your finances and keep the profits coming.

 5 Common Launch Errors You MUST Avoid!

1. **Insistence on autonomy**

In the startup phase, the company is all about you. Your fingerprints are on everything, and there is very little you don't know and aren't directing. But after the startup phase, the company streams into the growth phase, becoming more complex and more vulnerable to industry and economic trends. At that point, an entrepreneur's insistence on autonomy can hinder the company's ability to respond quickly and intelligently to challenges it faces.

2. Unwillingness to build structure

Many entrepreneurs will need to surround themselves with a strong executive team -- or at least a steady right-hand individual -- to ensure the company's success. But too many business owners fail to create the kind of structure that produces good leadership decisions within a managerial team. The entrepreneur needs to know the employees and where their strengths lie to put them to good use.

3. Lack of financial leadership

Entrepreneurs by definition take risk when they make the decision to start their own business. In the area of financial leadership, which includes tracking cash levels and trends, financial covenants, metrics and expenses, entrepreneurs who are not financially literate and active will need the direct support of a financial expert to ensure they receive the advice and input needed in their organization.

4. Reacting unwisely to boredom

Starting a business proved exhilarating. The day-to-day operation of it may pale in comparison. A bored entrepreneur can create significant troubles for the business. Things will get up-ended in a hurry, because many bored entrepreneurs either start new companies or abruptly make changes in their current company to keep their own level of excitement high.

5. Failure to engage in self-examination

Entrepreneurs need to be aware of their own strengths and weaknesses, the same things they engage in their employees.

 # 6 Tips to Rev Up Your Company This Year

As the owner of a startup or growing enterprise, if you are constantly stressing out and always in a state of flux, chances are that you are so busy working in your business that you are rarely working on your business. To be successful in business you can't get bogged down by day-to-day details. You must have your eyes set on the future. You have to be planning, strategizing, and building the best business in your industry. What is one thing all entrepreneurs can do to rev up their business this year?

Consider the following tips:

Use branded content.

If you think you still have "customers," you're wrong. You have an audience, and you need to build it. If you think you own your brand, you don't. You're newly created audience owns your brand. Give them the content they crave, and your company will flourish. So, throw out the old playbook and allow your branded content to drive your marketing.

Have brand ambassadors.

You need people at your company besides the founder who are credible. It shows online in the content that they produce and the events they speak at on a monthly basis. The way you brand them will help to gain trust and credibility online. Once you have someone's trust, you will have them as a customer for life.

Embrace lead intelligence and big data.

At this day and age, if you are not fully embracing lead intelligence and big data inside your organization, you're going to struggle. The availability of data to the SMB space has exploded over the past few years. The ease of integration into any CRM or marketing automation platform has brought big data into everyone's hands. If you don't take advantage of it, your competition will.

Gear quality leadership training toward millennial employees.

According to the Washington Post, 3.6 million baby boomers will retire, and more than one-fourth of the millennial workforce will move into a leadership role in 2016. This massive shift requires new types of training approached geared toward recruiting and retaining millennials. New leaders are flattening corporate management and focusing on social good, rather than just the bottom line.

You must prioritize.
Entrepreneurs often start with nothing, become adept at filling in cracks and being a jack of all trades. Over time that approach will hold the company back, and entrepreneurs need to regularly re-prioritize around their strengths. The focus should be on outsourcing all non-priority items into the organization. This makes the team stronger, avoids entrepreneur burnout, and accelerates growth.

Become more progressive.

The last few years have been about the expansion of digital tools, changes in marketing trends, and adopting advertising to new platforms, like streaming services, partnering with content creators, and developing relationships with up-and-coming thought leaders. Bear in mind that this year is truly about and refinement of those new core business facets, adopting them completely, and being progressive in your industry.

👉 You Must Read This to Improve Your Business Success!

The number of new business failures continues unabated. Here are the most common causes of failure you must avoid in order to improve your chances of success...

Lack of a Business Plan

You would think that anyone contemplating starting a business, considering the amount of time, effort and money involved, would develop a business plan, right? WRONG! The majority of new businesses are launched by entrepreneurs without a plan! Consequently, entrepreneurs get into trouble because they haven't considered all of the aspects associated with starting and managing a successful business.

Why is that? The typical entrepreneur (and his colleagues with whom he starts) is a "techie" of one type of another. I affectionately call them business innocents -- the founder and his soul brothers.

Many times, techies have never taken any courses on business (e.g. management, accounting, marketing, or planning). They are unaware of the fundamentals of what is required to run a business. And as a result, they experience a predictable series of natural pitfalls.

Insufficient Cash

Without a budget or even a break-even analysis, entrepreneurs rapidly squander their precious cash and waste valuable time. Entrepreneurs are long on ideas, but notoriously short on cash.

Entrepreneurs are very optimistic and perceive that everything will happen faster than is possible. In life -- as in business -- results usually take longer and costs more than expected.

Looking at their business with short-sighted time horizons, entrepreneurs expect to open their doors and become swamped with paying customers that will generate short-term cash and sustain the early stages of the business.

Unfortunately, even under the best circumstances, the typical start-up requires 18 to 24 months to generate positive cash flow. The statistics are well-known, and on average, 95% of all new businesses fail in the initial years of their existence.

You would also think that these well-published statistics would prompt entrepreneurs to plan better and have sufficient cash to fund their start-ups for at least the first year or more, right?

No Accounting Skills

Business is about numbers -- sales, costs, expenses, profits -- quantifiable transactions. If Wal-Mart knows what they sell in every store around the world, isn't that a strong indication of how critical it is to account for every aspect of your new business?

You can't manage what you don't know. Since entrepreneurs' dislike controls, have no budgets, and typically haven't done a break-even analysis, is it any surprise that so many new businesses fail? The simple fact is that it costs a certain amount of money to start almost any kind of business. So, the new business owner must calculate how much they must sell just to cover all costs and expenses they will inevitably incur, and by what date they must have them covered.

How many meals in the restaurant? How many bagels in the bagel shop? How many cupcakes in a Mr. Cupcakes? How many pizzas in a pizza parlor?

Everything about running a business is about numbers -- cash flow. If you don't keep track of every dollar spent and every dollar made in a timely fashion, then there can only be one result. Trouble!

Since CASH is KING, every penny needs to be accounted for in a proper fashion. Once you start your business, the money clocks start ticking. If you spend more than you generate, there can only be one outcome -- failure!

Lack of accounting controls, budgets and timely reporting of results is one of the major problems start-up businesses experience. Surprises can be deadly!

Selling vs. Marketing

Entrepreneurs are great salesmen. They are selling their idea for a better world. Unfortunately, they overestimate the number of customers that will find their solution applicable to them. Or they misinterpret the perceived worth of their value proposition. They also frequently misjudge how fast customers will adopt their solution. In addition, there are only so many hours to make sales in every day. Eventually, the typical entrepreneur runs out of time, energy, and resources.

Somewhere along the way, the typical entrepreneur has to realize that there are just not enough hours to sell, and they must transition their efforts from selling to marketing. Selling is asking for the order. Marketing is creating a demand in the mind of the customer so that they seek you out.

Poor People Skills

Management is simply getting things done through people. Entrepreneurs tend to be one man/woman shows. Running a successful business is a team effort.

The most successful firms constantly tout their people. They believe in every member of the team working together to deliver great products with excellent customer service.

The inability of the owner/founder to delegate authority and responsibility is another contributing factor to early demise of their business. Typical start-ups are helter skelter operations with everybody doing everything -- -including the founder. If allowed to continue, the only result can be chaos, confusion and the waste of precious resources.

When crisis management is the order of the day, failure isn't too far away. So, with no plan, insufficient cash, poor accounting controls, no organizational structure and a sell everything-to-everybody modus of operandi, what can the result be?

Remember: Nobody plans to fail...they just fail to plan.

A business plan is a relatively inexpensive exercise done on paper before you can start your business. It can save you from yourself!

How to Legally Protect Your Assets Once and For All!!

Most people can benefit immensely by utilizing a strategy that many entrepre-neurs and criminals alike have used for years. The strategy is based on two very simple principles: 1) A corporation is separate from the owner of the entity, and 2) The fact that true asset protection can only occur when the incentive to sue or in the case of criminal activity the opportunity for seizure is non-existent. Let's take a look at each of these points and then review the strategy to show you how everything works.

Corporations Are Separate from Their Owners

The most important thing to remember about any business entity is that it is separate from its owners. You are separate from your corporation, and your corporations are separate from one another. This is the very nature of the business entity, and it is the foundation upon which limited liability was built.

Because a corporation is an artificial person, you can do business with your corporation, and your corporation can do business with anyone else. This can include any other corporation you may own and or control. Your task in doing any type of multiple entity strategy is to maintain that separation. You separate you from your business by observing the rules of corporate formality, by keeping your corporate records clear and up to date. If we recognize that a corporation is not you, then we are half way home to understanding the terrific benefits of this strategy.

This brings us to the second major point in our strategy. Asset protection can only occur when your adversary has no incentive to sue you or your business. It also occurs when the IRS, FBI, or any other agency can't seize assets they allege belong to you during a criminal investigation. How do we accomplish such a lofty goal? Well, let's look at something that may seem a little strange; poverty. While this may sound silly, ask yourself this question: How many destitute people are on the wrong end of multi-million-dollar judgments? When was the last time you picked up the morning paper and saw a headline which read, "Joe Homeless sued for 5.5 million"? On the other hand, you read every day about someone with assets being sued, or large corporations being hauled into court. Is that because the homeless person never gets into trouble? Not at all! It is probably because "Joe Homeless" isn't worth suing! Think about it. Would you bother suing somebody who you knew couldn't possibly pay a judgment? Not likely in this day and age when most attorney's work on a contingency fee basis -- meaning they don't get paid unless there is something to take.

You may be thinking that it is all well and good to talk about using poverty as an asset protection tool, but poverty is no fun. You don't want to be poor. You own your own business, so you can have financial destiny. Well, in this case you are.

The Strategy

Keeping these two important points in mind, let's take a look at the strategy itself. The benefit of the strategy is you will be able to protect your business and personal assets from litigious attacks and seizures, and you might have the potential to reduce your taxes.

For purpose of this report, we are going to call your home-state business 123, Inc. The other corporation in our example is going to be called ABC, Inc. ABC, Inc. is a corporation that will be formed in Nevada to provide a service to 123, Inc.

123, Inc. Takes A Loan

Let's say that your 123, Inc. corporation goes to the bank and borrows a significant amount of money. The bank is going to want collateral to guarantee repayment. Let's say that your corporation is required to offer all of its assets as collateral for the loan, and is then required to pay large sums of interest on the note, so large that it may have difficulty even making the payments. Therefore, 123, Inc. would always be in debt, and if the payments aren't made the bank can take everything 123, Inc. owns and pledged as collateral to re-pay the note. In essence, 123, Inc. could be wiped out. Perfect! Who would want to sue such a company?

Nobody, because even if they won, the bank gets paid off first, and then there's little likelihood of having anything left. Again, this accomplished the goal of "removing the incentive to be sued", but who wants to be in debt? Unless, of course, you were in control of the bank!

It is very possible through very proper planning and structuring that you can have your cake and eat it too. How? Because if the lending company was your own ABC, Inc. corporation, you have protected everything you own! You now have a home state corporation that has a terrible debt and is unattractive to any adversary's lawsuit. But at the same time, you are calling all of the shots with its creditor. You have the best of both worlds. Even if somebody does sue 123, Inc., and obtains a judgment, what are they going to get? The same thing they would get if they sued "Joe Homeless" -- only headaches. You, on the other hand, are in the driver's seat. Even if you do not win the lawsuit you are judgment proof because ABC, Inc. is the bank. You have total control over it, and you decide what happens if 123, Inc. can't pay its interest, and you decide what happens if someone tries to take your assets from 123, Inc.

Remember that ABC, Inc. has the first lien on everything. Anybody trying to get at the assets at 123, Inc. must pay ABC, Inc. off first.

There's one more little detail we need to cover here, and that is paying interest on the loan made from ABC, Inc. This is a real loan, requiring a set interest rate to be set. Of course, interest on the loan is tax deductible and this would be true in 123, Inc.'s home state. But, if ABC, Inc. were in an income tax free state such a Nevada, how much income tax will it have to pay to its state? None! Thus, the more interest you can pay on the note, the more income you will move from your home state.

Summary

In short, the strategy involves two corporations. The first is your primary business, and for our example we called it 123, Inc. The other company will be a Nevada corporation, which we have called ABC, Inc.
123, Inc. borrows money from ABC, Inc. and as a result goes into debt. ABC, Inc. takes all of the assets of 123, Inc. as collateral for the loan, and files the necessary documents to perfect its security interest, such as UCC-1 financing statements for personal property, and mortgages or Deeds of Trust for any real estate. 123, Inc. pays interest to ABC, Inc. which reduces its state income tax, and ABC, Inc. has a first position on the assets of 123, Inc., making it a very unattractive lawsuit or seizure target.

That, in a nutshell, is the ABC-123 strategy.

Best Advice from 15 Self-Made Millionaires!

Rick Alden, founder of Skullcandy: "The fastest route to revenue wins." Coming up with ideas is never a problem for a creative team. Instead, the challenge is learning to say no to nine great ideas to free up the resources to push one product to market immediately. "The one product may not be your fantasy, but revenue on a simpler product today always beats running out of money developing a more complicated product that won't launch for another year."

Sheila Johnson, founder and CEO of Salamaner Hotels & Resorts: "Surround yourself with a great team, and build that team slowly. Your team is one of your most important investments, and if you are careful about hiring only the best people, it will pay dividends."

Peter Relan, founder of 9+: "It's all about the sailor." No matter how great an

The Cell Block Presents TCB University

idea is, success in business is more about the sailor than the boat. "A great entrepreneur can take a bad idea and turn it into something incredible. This means that, while ideas are important, it's even more critical to have the right people in the right positions to execute them."

Melinda Emerson, founder and CEO of Quintessence Group: "Always know your next hire." There are countless risks associated with being a small-business owner, and one of the biggest is staffing. "Nobody is going to love your business as much as you do, so you have to protect it." People will quit on the worst day possible -- so long as it's advantageous for them. "Keep in touch with people you didn't hire but you really liked; you never know when you might need to call upon them to help you out."

Jim Murren, chairman and CEO of MGM Resorts International: "Spend most of your time looking forward." You need to have the capacity to envision the long term. "Creating teams that have an understanding of not only what they are doing, but why they are doing it, it critical."

Christine Day, CEO of Luvo: "If you wait for evidence, you'll be a follower, not a leader." You cannot rely on market research for innovation. "There is no evidence for what has not been created yet; only insight, purpose, passion and a willingness to move into what could be instead of what is. Truly innovative companies are not afraid to let go and create the next market shift."

Diane Bryant, senior vice president and GM of Data Center Group, Intel: "There is value in expanding and rounding out your expertise skill set." Just because you've been around the block doesn't mean you can't grow as a professional. "The better you understand your customer, the higher the probability of success." Learn firsthand what works and what doesn't.

Nick Lazaris, president and CEO of Corvan: "Trust yourself. In business, you have to act on your instincts because, ultimately, you will be the one who is responsible. If your decision fails, it ought to be something you really believed in. You want to be able to own up to it and learn from it."

Peter Thum, founder and CEO of Liberty United: "Choose to do the right thing. As an entrepreneur, you always will face adversity. You can't predict what that adversity will be, but if you try to do the right thing, and that right thing is based on a set of values you keep, ultimately you will come out well."

Shama Hyder, CEO and founder of Marketing Zen: "The first idea is rarely the best one." Ideas are like the people who have them -- always changing, always getting better. "Most businesses start with what they think is a great idea, but in almost every case, the ideas change over time. In the past, business success used to be about having a bulletproof long-term strategy; now it's all about the ability to stay agile and adapt." The takeaway is simple: Constantly evaluate.

Josh Elman, partner of Greylock Partners: "Don't take calls -- make calls. It's up to you to make things happen. So much of what happens in the world of business is inbound -- you react to this, you field that. In reality, especially when you've decided to follow a passion, you should take matters into your own hands and push things outbound."

Khajak Keledjian, co-founder and chief executive of Intermix: "Focus on what makes you different. Creativity is to see what everyone else sees but think of what nobody else thought of. Focusing on that point of view, focusing on what makes you different, really is the most important way to stand out in the marketplace."

Rehan Choudhry, founder of Life is Beautiful: "Stop being scared, and jump. What makes an entrepreneur is not knowing everything about business, but rather being passionate and fearless. There's no 'right time' to take the leap; you can take it at any point in your life and should." Don't overthink every decision or opportunity that comes your way. Stay focused and nimble.

Reece Pacheco, founder of Shelby.tv: "Be human." It's easy to focus on transactions, especially when you're struggling to start a company. But this is when it's most important to remember that your customers are people, too. "Take a second to recognize that there is a person on the other side of you. It can make all the difference in the world."

Kim Graham-Nye, co-founder and president of gDiapers: "Be sure to take care of yourself. We need to break the myth around 'balance' and create a new paradigm for understanding and valuing our time, our passions, and our priorities in order to be our greatest selves."

 The 6 Entrepreneurial Profiles!

Researchers have identified traits and personality profiles that appear to correlate

to success in business. Among them:
Professional experience. The average candidate is 34 years old and has domain and management experience.

Fluid intelligence. This genetic trait is also referred to as "abstract thinking." Successful founders who demonstrate this trait are able to recognize patterns and quickly learn rule sets, then apply them quickly to solve problems.
Openness. Creativity, curiosity and a desire to seek new experiences and knowledge are desirable traits.

Moderate agreeableness. The best founders exude a sense of compassion and are generally warm and considerate -- but are capable of being straightforward or even harsh when necessary.

Varying degrees of these and other traits were used to compile the six basic entrepreneurial profiles. Where do you fit in?
Exuding confidence, HUSTLERS (aka "go-getter salespeople") are enthusiastic, action-oriented and conscientious, never lacking in self-discipline and follow-through. They score 25 percent above average in both extraversion and conscientiousness. They are highly agreeable individuals, always interested in the needs of others.
Examples: Mary Kay Ash, Zig Ziglar

The quintessential disruptors, INNOVATORS ("caring thinkers") are adventurous forward-thinking and always on the look-out for unconventional business ideas. They score high in openness (creativity and inventiveness) and agreeability but are slightly below average in terms of emotional stability.
Examples: Richard Branson, Tony Hsieh, Evan Williams

Those who always get the job done and on time are MACHINES ("quiet, diligent doers"). These people have a strong sense of duty and an aptitude for problem-solving. Machines score 80 percent above average in conscientiousness and 10 percent above average in fluid intelligence; where they are lacking slightly is in openness, the search for new ideas.
Examples: Larry Ellison, Bill Gates

Gifted with inherent business sense, PRODIGIES ("stoic, brilliant recluses") run on instinct, trusting in their natural intellect and social skills to succeed. Prodigies score high in fluid intelligence, agreeability and emotional stability.
Examples: Elon Musk, Larry Page

Creative tacticians, STRATEGISTS ("somewhat difficult, creative ops") rely on their intellect to develop effective business models and to never lose their cool. They score 55 percent above the norm in emotional stability and also demonstrate openness and high fluid intelligence.
Examples: Steve Jobs, Martha Stewart

Always perceptive to their demographic, VISIONARIES ("uber-creatives") see the big picture and constantly try to push their companies to new heights. That enthusiasm leads to a high score -- 40 percent above average -- in extraversion, as well as above-average ratings in openness and fluid intelligence.
Examples: Ted Turner, Oprah Winfrey, Mark Zuckerberg

BO$$ Status: A Guide to Entrepreneurial Leadership!

When I think of the best leadership, I am moved and humbled. Great leaders inspire and create meaningful, lasting opportunities and new ways of thinking. They believe in change. They have an impact on the future.

Like many roles in life and business, being a true leader is a calling. Either you're a great one, or you're not. Think of those who have changed the expected, like Picasso, Plato, Thelma and Louise, Socrates and Tom Brady.

Those are the ones that blaze new trails without fear, without worry and without a second thought to what other people think. They have a singular vision and a singular course. They dare to challenge ideas with a nimble flick of the throttle, changing directions as easily as batting an eye. They see things others do not. They take risks. They are entrepreneurs. Just like you. And if you doubt that fact, sit back and have a read.

Leadership is your contribution and your service to your company. It's your survival, and that of those you lead. It will be your legacy, and your company's legacy. It is what makes you great versus what lets you fail or, worse, be average.

Ask anyone in the armed forces -- especially those operating in the battlefield -- about leadership, and they will be telling. It's usually along the lines of: "I am leading you to keep you alive. I lead for you, and I lead to make you better."

The point is: Leadership is never about you -- it's about them. And how you lead says a lot about your company and a lot about you. And if you're not good at it... damn, that's bad.

Those who are true leaders will lead their teams to victory and inspire them to be great. I've worked with that type, and I've worked with leaders who are managers and mostly check timecards. The difference is epic. Leadership is not about bossing or being in control. Nope. It is that belief that you and your team are destined for something special. It is your ability to inspire excellence in others.

Any organization, company, product, magazine or brand will always, always, every single time, take on the essence of its leader. If you lead with courage, clarity and fearlessness, then that's what your brand will stand for. The same goes if you are a careless, hopeless, entitled brat.
I've succeeded, and I've failed as a leader. And the lesson is this: When you lead with purpose and vision, you will succeed. When you lead out of fear, you will fail.

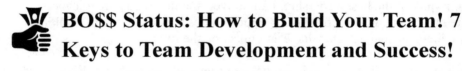 BO$$ Status: How to Build Your Team! 7 Keys to Team Development and Success!

Being a phenomenal leader isn't about the leader -- it's about the team. To create a successful and innovative team, you need to be flexible and able to collaborate with team members who may be your complete opposite. It's about finding their strengths and focusing on how to leverage their unique talents to improve the entire team.

Here are the seven keys for team development you should keep in mind to ensure the success of your team:

Thoughtful Recruiting.

The process of recruiting new team members cannot be rushed. To find the best employees for your team, you need to first determine your business' unique needs. Then, you should refuse to settle until you find the perfect fit between your company and a potential employee. It can help to develop specific competencies that your next hire needs to possess. Establishing these criteria, before you accept applications and interview all candidates several times to ensure they fill the needs of the position, are essential to the team-building process.

Initial Training.

As a leader, you should make the development of individual team members your top priority. Leading is more than teaching the mechanics of a role. You should show your enthusiasm and teach your employees how to maintain high-energy attitudes. Business school teaches the rules, but it doesn't teach how to be a top producing or innovative employee. You may consider designing a proprietary training program that's progressive and hands-on. Your employees already have the professionalism and passion, they just need to learn the correct mentality and receive support while they build the business.

Promoting Collaboration.

All of your team members have unique strengths and weaknesses. Use them to your advantage.
By placing each team member in a position that harnesses strengths and downplays weaknesses, you ensure that everyone is successful and able to reach their full potential within the team. Leverage your talent pool to its peak productivity and encourage collaboration. This is the key to innovation.

Having A Passion for People.

Value your people more than the processes. Have fun. Get out of the office! Celebrate your employees' work and their personal successes. Once you understand your team members and what they enjoy, you'll start to feel like a family.

Consistent Coaching.

Coaching your team goes beyond training. It's an ongoing conversation that will continuously
increase productivity and team engagement. Meet with your team and individual employees regularly, either weekly or monthly, to ensure you are identifying obstacles or opportunities as they arise and addressing them directly. Dangle the carrot in front of your team. Keep energy high by creating goals of achievement for additional possibilities.

Maintaining Accountability.

Once you create goals for your team, clearly communicate your expectations. For example, ask your team members to work to their strengths while focusing on the top 20 percent of their most impactful and income-generating activities. Holding yourself and your team accountable to these standards will keep you on track while making you more relatable.

Leading by Example.

Strive to intentionally make a difference in your team members' careers. Be deliberate. If business is slow and calls need to be made, don't be afraid to do the hard things to encourage others. It takes cognitive control and discipline to bring positive energy to the table every day, but it will pay off and your reputation will thank you. Focus on productivity and profitability and remember: high-impact priorities lead to critical advantages.

The team development process isn't over once you hire your dream employees. Building an innovative and collaborative company requires an on-going commitment to your individual team members. Bring a high-energy attitude to the table every day and encourage your team members to do the same. If you encourage them and put your trust in them, they will deliver for you and your bottom line.

Remember, to be a successful leader, you must inspire your team to greatness. If you motivate them to be great, they will take care of your company. Develop a positive workplace culture and you won't have to worry about your employees. They will reward you and take care of your bottom line.

Bo$$ Status: How to Encourage Your Team!

Encouragement. It sounds like such a small thing. Subtle. Cute. It's what we do with timid kittens.

But encouragement isn't cute -- it's fraught and powerful. When you're encouraging, you're instilling courage. That's huge. And that's hard. And its way more compelling than motivation.

Motivation doesn't depend on circumstances. Motivation is for people who are already inclined to try to succeed.

The commencement addresses that go viral are always more encouraging that they are motivational. The speakers recognize a specific concern -- like needing to get a job or facing an uncertain future -- and discuss ways it can be overcome.

GET MONEY: Self-Educate, Get Rich & Enjoy Life, Vol. 1

They don't offer some vague challenge like "surmounting an obstacle" or "seizing upon your dreams" or "surmounting your dreams by seizing upon an obstacle" or whatever the current motivational clichés are. Do these addresses involve motivation? Yes. Are they "motivational" in that unctuous way that motivational things are? No. Commencement addresses make listeners accountable. Encouragement inherently involves accountability -- and not just for the one being encouraged. The encourager is accountable, too.

How to Encourage...

Praise the actual. If you read all the research on motivation, it pretty much comes down to this: Praise works better then criticism.
We all have an emotional tank. It works like the gas tank of a car. There has to be way more tank-filling than tank-draining.

Acknowledge the potential. Encouragement involves the acknowledgement of a negative thing -- that the people being encouraged don't know they're not doing (or trying to do) but you think they should be doing. They might think they're doing just fine, that they're being appropriately effective and ambitious. Encouragement often involves bursting a confidence bubble.
To be encouraging, you must believe two things to be true. One, the person is not trying hard enough, which is probably not something the person wants to hear; and two, if the person tried, he or she could do great things, which is good. The key to encouraging is to deliver the bad news in a way that doesn't force the person to dwell on inadequacies. The key to encouragement is tact.

Start off by telling them their strong points and acknowledging their efforts and talents. 'You're extremely creative and you're brilliant, and you're wonderful at coming up with new ideas.' And then from there you can say, 'I would love to see you be able to segue that into a more organized manner.' It's very easy for people to kind of lose track of what they're doing right and what they're doing wrong.

Challenge specifically. You motivate generally. But you must encourage specifically. This holds the person accountable. "You should ask this person for help." "You should go after that job." "You should consider switching to this career." Like that.
For example, 'I think you have the potential to be a fantastic leader and to have three people work under you...but to do that, I think we need to improve upon your time-management skills, your organizing skills,' vs. coming at them saying, 'You're disorganized.' Approach it from a potential route.

Why It Matters...

Encouragement means empowerment. A lot of time it comes down to guide autonomy. So, on one hand, we know from research that people are much better at work when they feel empowered, which consists of having meaning on the job, a sense of autonomy, a sense of confidence, and also an impact on what you do and the people you're trying to help. Yet you don't want to feel so autonomous that you have no direction. It's one thing to feel autonomous in terms or your motivation, but it's another thing to be autonomous and go in the wrong direction.

You have to discourage before you encourage. That challenge is scary -- for both parties. But the reward is sweet. Not only have you helped someone achieve a goal; you've helped someone achieve a goal that he or she didn't previously have. That's not merely motivational -- that's magical. You're a wizard, a coach, a seer and (if we're being honest) kind of pain, all at the same time.

Key Technical Matters...

Encouragement has two parts: pointing out potential and challenging the person to succeed at a specific goal.

You have to point out what it is to believe the other person could do. And you have to challenge him or her to do it. Which is why it's so much more meaningful than motivation.

You can motivate anyone. You can encourage only someone you actually believe in.

Encouragement requires specificity.

You don't encourage someone to succeed. (That's motivation.) You encourage someone to succeed at a specific task or job.

You don't encourage people to "do it." You encourage people to do that thing you think they are prepared to do but has never occurred to them.

Behind every successful person is someone who said: "You should try this. I think you'd be good at it. And here's how you should try."
That last part is important. Encouragement without guidance isn't encouragement. It's discouragement. "Here's what you're not doing! Bye!"

When you encourage, you don't just change how people work. You change the way they perceive their abilities. Which changes their careers. Which changes their lives. Which is a really big deal.

BO$$ Status: How to Be a Better Boss

Learn How to Effectively Delegate with These 8 Easy to Follow Steps

One of the great things about being a boss is that you can delegate various types of tasks to other people instead of having to do them yourself. This may sound like a rather cavalier statement, but it's true. As a manager, to do your job efficiently and effectively, you must delegate various types of tasks to your staff. If you don't delegate, you will be overworked, and your staff will be underutilized. In fact, you do a disservice to your staff if you don't delegate because this inhibits your staff's ability to learn new things and grow as professionals.

Like all management activities, delegation must be done in a thoughtful, ethical and forward-thinking manner. To that end, consider the following tips when delegating tasks to your staff, contractors, vendors and others.

Clearly define what can and cannot be delegated.

As a boss, be mindful of what should and should not be delegated. For example, specific tasks may contain proprietary information that should not be shared at your staff's organizational level. There are also tasks that your team members may not be qualified to perform, thus setting them up for failure. Lastly, don't just dump unwanted activities onto your staff to get them off your plate. Your team will eventually figure this out and it will hurt your credibility as their manager.

Delegation in a powerful tool to maximize your team's productivity, enhance their skill set, help them grow professionally and free you up to perform higher level tasks. All that said -- make sure you are delegating the right tasks for the right reasons.

Create a prioritized delegation plan.

Now knowing what to delegate, your next step is to develop a plan outlining what tasks should be delegated to which staff member. When determining who

gets which tasks, you should consider the following:
Who is fully qualified to perform the task?

Who could perform the task with proper instruction and mentoring with the goal of enhancing their skill set?

Who should not be given the task because of their professional weaknesses?

Who deserves the task based on seniority, past performance and relevant considerations?
The visibility and importance of the task to your department and/or company. Delegating the right tasks to the right people is not always easy or popular, but if you do it with transparency, fairness, consistency, and for the good of the company, your staff will learn to respect your decisions.

Provide clear instructions.

There is nothing worse than being delegated a task, not given instructions on how the task should be performed, not told what is expected, working diligently to complete the task, and then being told it isn't what they wanted. Give specific instructions as to what needs to be done and your expectation of the ending result. This combination of instructions and expectations provides the correct delegation framework and establishes criteria as to how your employee will be judged when the task is completed.

Provide a safety net.

When delegating tasks -- particularly if it's a new experience for the employee being assigned the task -- as the boss, you must be willing to provide an appropriate level of management support to help assure success, for both the employee and the task.

A safety net is an environment of help and protection by:
Providing the needed resources.
Allowing time to perform the tasks.
Helping employees navigate company politics.
Provide instructions on how tasks should be performed.

Let go and allow people to do their work.

If you delegate a task and then micro-manage it to the extent that you have actually performed the task yourself, it's not delegation. Neither should you totally divest yourself from the delegated task because, as the boss, you are still ultimately responsible for all work performed within your department. The trick is to walk that fine line between being overbearing and non-participatory.

Be mentoring and instructive.

This step provides direct instruction and advice to the person performing a specific delegated task. This type of task-based instruction is a "learning moment," namely, just in time training on how to perform a specific task or how to deal with a specific situation.

The level of instruction and advice to be provided should be based on the combination of the person's specific experience and the task difficulty and political ramifications.

Give credit to those doing the work.

As a boss, you should adhere to the philosophy of "it's the team's success or my failure." This philosophy causes you to raise the visibility of your staff's good work within the organization which is motivating them and helps instill loyalty in your staff toward you.

This approach also helps remind you that you are ultimately responsible for both your team's growth and your department's productivity and performance.

Actively solicit feedback from your team.

Asking the members of your team if they believe you have delegated the right tasks to the right people has the following advantages:

Helps you grow as a boss/manager by learning how you are perceived as one. Helps improve your team's performance by providing you with insights on better ways to delegate.

BO$$ Status: 3 Easy Step to Better Leadership!

As a business owner, you rely on your leadership team to coach, train and support your workforce to help your company grow and prosper.

An ability to understand individual styles and model your culture will help your leaders be a resource for your employees' personal and professional growth. It's not easy, but the payoff of an engaged, productive workforce will be worth it.

Here are three areas where your leadership team can get started...

Know Your Culture

If your company culture isn't what you'd anticipated, it's not too late to rescue it. Start by asking:

How well do your employees enjoy their work? Coming to work shouldn't be feelings of dread.

Is there a level of accountability and responsibility? Taking ownership makes employees feel connected.

Are your employees engaged? Believing what they do matters to the company and its mission leads to committed employees.

How do you invest in your employees? Recognition for a job well done shows that you value your team's work.

Build Relationships

The better you and your leadership knows your employees, the better position you'll all be in to help them, and the company, continue to succeed.

How to develop lasting relationships:
Look at things from their perspective.
Earn respect and trust by being open and real.
Be their advocate and help them develop.
Be open to input from your employees.
Give them latitude to solve problems.

Foster Independence

Your leadership team can nurture self-guided success by creating a culture of independent thinking and creativity.

Spell out expectations and guidelines up front, but trust employees to execute their work creatively.
Expect some failures. They're part of the process.

Deal with issues individually rather than implementing companywide policies to address a single situation.
Promote work-life balance. Provide opportunities for professional development.

BO$$ Status: Focus on The Vision!

When was the last time you remember bringing your absolute "A Game" to your small business, decisions and relationships? It's likely that your memories are either too distant or too infrequent to feel satisfying. Given the rapidly changing environments within which we live and work, "overwhelmed" and "stretched too thin" are common sentiments. The irony is that during a time when most are desperately in pursuit of creativity, innovation and emotionally intelligent leadership, there is a simultaneous pushing of our employees and ourselves to exhaustion -- depletion of the very sources most needed.

There is a new way of approaching work and time that allows for more efficient allocation of resources and strategic outcomes: focus management. Focus management begins with investment in self, first, to rejuvenate the body and mind. Strategic leaders are typically more attuned to themselves holistically. They care about wellness, take longer or more regular vacations, find ways to unwind doing something that is joyful, and have diverse interests and relationships. Even though a holistic approach seems like common sense, many professionals report feeling that investing in downtime seems luxurious. On the contrary, research clearly shows that rejuvenated leaders are more attentive to the subtle cues in the environment, willing to hear divergent points of view and adept in coaching employees.

Understand the Vision

Focus management begins with a clear understanding of the vision. Where are you trying to go? Where are you trying to take your team? Your organization? A vision is a compelling and end state -- an inspired-for destination. Vivid means that you should be able to close your eyes and see the vision in detail, including seeing yourself in it. A compelling vision is one that is so enticing that you cannot help but act in a way that brings it into being. It is powerful enough to stimulate energy that makes you literally jump out of bed in the morning, or stay up all night, or do whatever it takes to make it a reality.

In the absence of a compelling vision, people tend to focus primarily on fear --

the "what ifs" associated with not having a clear sense of the future. The energy used is called distress, or negative emotional stress. Stressful energy is what we use to worry; it is emotionally exhausting.

It is important to remember that humans are wired to have emotional responses. Emotions that focus on fear are able to cause distress. Emotions that focus on vision are able to stimulate eustress, a creative energy.

Establish Creative Tension

The work of leaders is to maximize the opportunity for eustress in the workplace. This is done by keeping the vision firmly in focus and fleshing out the path to the vision through strategic planning and use of other analytical frameworks. Tapping into this creative tension enhances one's ability to broadly explore ideas from multiple perspectives and build capacity for addressing other complex issues in the future. It also allows for criteria-driven prioritization of activities that are aligned with the vision. Ultimately, people throughout your organization develop comfort and confidence identifying and choosing strategic investments over "putting out fires."
Put it into Practice

As an example of how to begin this shift in focus, make a list of 10 things you do at work on a weekly basis that you think make the biggest contribution to: 1) the strategic goals of your small business organization, 2) your colleagues, and 3) your clients. Next, label each item with a T for Task, M for Management or L for Leadership. Tasks are things you do in reaction mode. They are typically detail oriented and require you to be hands-on with their" completion. Management responsibilities are focused on developing stronger skills and confidence in people and efficiently allocating and leveraging resources. Management is balancing fast-paced troubleshooting with slower, more reflective attention to ensuring solid processes are in place. Leadership involves anticipating and then facilitating toward to a desired future. Leadership behaviors often involve taking risks, exerting influence, environmental scanning and positioning yourself, your team or organization to advance identified goals.

Look at your distribution of T, M and Ls. Are there too many Ts and not enough Ls? If yes, it's likely because doing the work of leadership -- learning, reflecting, analyzing, positioning -- does not always appear busy enough. Strategic leaders balance T, M and Ls rather than being pulled in the busy trap. Putting out fires is often emotionally draining. It solves an immediate problem but does. not necessarily resolve issues to prevent them from resurfacing in the future; the return on investment is minimal.

Strategic leaders create, articulate, and advance a shared vision that enables prioritization of long-term sustainable efforts, versus time- and crisis management.

How One Guy Made $20 Million In Under A Year... and YOU Can, TOO!

Wayne White, a fat guy many of you may remember being on your TV screens at the wee hours of the morning with a half-hour infomercial, made tens of millions doing just what we are talking about here, but even he didn't make up this idea. White got the idea from a writer of a book on mail order marketing named Ted Nicholas. Nicholas himself had made millions on the same basic idea ten years earlier. Looking for a product he could market, he discovered that the US government during World War Two had commissioned many excellent foreign language instruction books and made "native speaker" phonograph records to teach languages to soldiers being sent to those areas as translators and intelligence gatherers. Nicholas copied the books, packaged the recordings on tape cassettes, and wrote a famous ad: "Speak Spanish like a Diplomat!" He sold many "Linguaphone" language home study kits, and eventually sold this business to another marketing organization for several million dollars.

After reading Ted's story in a "how to get rich quick" book, White himself visited a US Government Printing Office store in his home town and took a total of two hours to discover that the US government had zillions of brochures on sale for a few dollars each. Many outlined the details of hundreds of programs involving low interest government loans and grants. He gathered up all the low cost or free brochures on this subject, had them bound and then reprinted them into his own book. He called the finished product, Free Money: Government Loans and Grants by Nevada White. Price? $49.95! For a member of the public, it would have cost perhaps $75 to buy these pamphlets individually at the Government Book Shop, and it would take work to select, index and organize them logically. White handled these details and was able to print and bind the material into a paperback costing him less than $3 per copy. He even got government loans and grants to fund his new publishing business. His main objective was to sell these books with material he obtained free, and to promote a live seminar based on them.

Over the years, later editions of his book included reader success stories and testimonials. The book cost him about $4 to print and mail. He got a low rate on mailing as he declared himself to be a non-profit educational organization. White got free advertising by appearing on late night radio or TV talk shows discussing the topic, "FREE MONEY." After he had sold several thousand copies this way, he filmed an "infomercial" to promote the idea of applying grants and loans. This was an original and new idea for selling his book.

It didn't take long for any up-front funding to get these infomercials played again and again on late night TV. Free running time has obtained by making participation deals: The broadcasting station ran White's video tape and provided an order taking service. It was paid a third of the gross on every sale. With a nominal cost, a sales price of $50, less a commission of $16, and fulfilment costs of $4 that still left nearly $30 on each sale for profit. Two million FREE MONEY books were sold in six months. That's how White made his first million. Like most people who make money too fast, he spent too much and ultimately lost it all, but that's another story. The point is, here is a writer who couldn't write (did I forget to mention he was illiterate?!), a jazz drummer who took someone else's idea, got a free product, and became the highest paid author in the world back in 1988.

Can you, do it? Maybe. What is the concept? Find a topic that people like to read about, then create a product yourself, or get it for free somewhere.

Topic suggestions: Making Money, Getting More and Better Sex, Pet Training, Cooking, Dieting, Avoiding Taxes, Learning Anything, Celebrity Secrets, Success, or just about anything. Then get the material together in a sensible order, and put it between two covers, on a CD or DVD. It doesn't have to be original.

After the FREE MONEY book, White got a collection of recipes from parishioners at a certain church who had put the anthology together to raise money for the church. The church's production cost of 200 copies of an offset-printed cookbook with binding was about $2 each. The church's fund-raising auxiliary sold them for $5.

White took the recipes and replaced the church's cover with a much nicer one and had the book professionally printed. His cost per book was closer to $1.75 each on a press run of 2000 copies and his sales price was $19.95. The book made more money for him than it did for the church, but the church was happy with the deal White gave them. He traded the lady at the church 100 printed copies for sale at the church in exchange for the right to use the recipes forever. As you can see his cost for the material was his printing cost on 100 books -- $175. Thanks to clever ads and promotion the book did very well for him. A percentage of his mailing list (those who bought FREE MONEY) also bought cookbooks. These days, you can also put together and market CDs and DVDs.

Everything written here should spark your imagination. You come up with the product and marketing variations. Material that has been around a long time is usually free of copyright restrictions. This is why you see a collection of old songs/hits being hyped on TV by people who had no connection to the singer or original composer. The people marketing this material pay them nothing. Old movies such as Jimmy Stewart's classic, You Only Live Once are in the public domain. By computer coloring this movie, a complete outsider was able to copyright the new colored version, and make an excellent return renting the movie to TV stations to play. I just watched a movie, Heart of the Sea, which was the Moby Dick story. Moby Dick is in the public domain. There's a TV show on titled Sleepy Hollow. It's based on a book from the same name, which is in the public domain. You might be surprised at what you can find in the public domain and bring back to life for today's generation.

The trick? Get your product either cheap or for free. Look for something that you like. If you like it, odds are other people will, too. All you have to do is write a good ad. Ads can be placed in free ad papers, on bulletin boards, or dropped in mailboxes or placed under doors. With practice, you can get free publicity and can appear on radio and TV shows to promote your product. Maybe you can do an infomercial, too.

The general public has the idea from movies and TV shows that every writer or artist laboriously creates something original and then a publisher or promoter buys it or agrees to pay royalties. The reality is that, for every dollar an author gets on such deals, other authors better at self-marketing are getting hundreds more for their books, CDs, films and products via mail order and other non-conventional means. What is sold in conventional bookstores is probably less than five percent of gross revenues for these products.

Scope International, a privately-owned mail order publisher in England, had more sales volume than all the bookstores in a medium-sized city combined. And Scope is just one of many such outfits started by one man. Originally an author of books about collecting plates and ceramic mugs, he got fed up with rejection slips. He decided to self-publish, market his own material, and began to make deals with other authors.

Before he sold out, the rental fees he received for his mailing lists alone were more than many small publishers earn, and certainly more than all but a few published authors make. Another advantage of self-marketing is that a major publisher will promote any book with advertising and publicity only for a few months. No matter how good it is or how well it sells, a regular publisher's attention always turns to new books. Thus, conventionally published books go out of print and are remaindered, i.e. discounted at close-out sales, and quickly forgotten. In contrast, a self-publisher can sell updated, revised and expanded editions of his book forever. There are always new generations coming along and the market is so big that it can never be saturated.

How A TEEN Averages $2,800 In Monthly Profits!

As a child, Anna Erkalova made her first foray into small business by selling handmade soaps to her mother's friends. But during her junior year in high school, the avid reader and resident of Chalfont, Pennsylvania, came up with a bigger and better idea: starting her own publishing company, Crane Books LLC, to bring old literary works into the eBook era. "It's like I'm giving the books a new life by making them more easily available," Erkalova says.

Her niche is publishing public domain literature -- books that have an expired copyright -- that is out of print or unavailable in electronic form. Her titles range from Lord of the Flies author William Golding's lesser-known The Inheritors to Solomon Northup's memoir Twelve Year's a Slave, which inspires the 2013 acclaimed film. For each title, she purchases a physical copy of the book, scans each page, and uploads the electronic file to websites such as Amazon and Barnes & Noble. She sells about 100 books a month, making around $2,800 in monthly profits, and to date has donated more than $2,000 of her proceeds to charity.

Anna's idea is tremendously creative and very much with the times, using technology and new ways of reading. She definitely found a need and came up with a product for it. She has a great entrepreneurial spirit and has a bright future ahead of her.

Her biggest challenge? The monotony of scanning and upholding each book, a process that takes around 12 hours. "I read along with the book as I scan it, though, so that keeps me entertained," she says.

Erkalova now attends Princeton University, where she majors in chemical and biological engineering and plans to keep running -- and growing -- her business with help from her classmates. "I'll meet a lot of really smart, ingenious people at Princeton," she says. "I'm interested to see what [business ideas] we come up with."

If she can do it, why can't you? Get money!

How to Make Money Doing Internet Info Searches for Inmates!

The worldwide web contains a vast amount of information virtually free to anyone who wants it. With google and other online subject locators, you can find just about anything you want within seconds or minutes!

Well, unless you're an inmate ... Because inmates don't have Internet success! This is where a money-making opportunity for you comes in. Inmates, isolated from the outside world, are constantly in need of information. Whether it's for a book they're writing, case they're working on, correspondence course they're taking, some kind of entertainment they're looking for or any other kind of resource needed, you can offer your Internet info search service and charge a fee. All for googling information that's free to you, then printing and mailing it to inmates.

Prices for this kind of service ranges, but for example purposes, an average price is $5.00 per topic searched, up to 10 pages of black and white results, and $6.50 for up to 10 pages of color results. Additional pages are typically 20¢ each for black and white and 35¢ for color.

Legal research is typically more expensive. Things like case law is typically $3.75 per case for up to 10 pages, 20¢ per additional page, and case law sherardizing is $3.75 for the first citation for up to 10 pages, 20¢ per additional page, and $2.50 for each additional citation needed. Legal research in need of using online resources like LexisNexis, legal magazines and newspapers, professional websites, etc.? $25 per hour, one hour minimum, plus 10¢ per printed page! $25.00 per hour for sitting at home on your computer in a soft chair and air-conditioned room is not a bad gig. Need more examples? How's this:

Many inmates are looking for a long-lost family member, friend or witness. For a basic person/people search you can charge $4 for one, $7 for two, $10 for three, etc. But some companies charge as much as $10-$20 for one person! While you, too, can charge this, it may be best to keep your price(s) competitive.

And did you know prisoners are always looking for someone to print song lyrics?

Prisoners are always looking for lyrics they can write and send to their special someone, or to songs that bring back memories of a better time, so they can rap or sing them on the tier. You can charge inmates an average of $1.25 a song, or $5.00 for 5!

As you can see, you can make extra money providing Internet searches for inmates. And if you have a computer and printer, you've got everything you need to provide the service, all you need to do now is get the word out by advertising to the inmate population. There are several effective ways to do this. You can get a free listing of 75 words or less in The BEST Resource Directory for Prisoners, 'an inmate favorite, by sending your text ad to thecellblock.net@mail.com. If you want a bigger, display ad, contact them for their current prices. You can contact Diane, CEO of Freebird Publishers at Diane@FreebirdPublishers.com and ask about a listing in her Inmate Shopper, another resource directory for prisoners. And you can also advertise in the Prison Legal News. PLN boasts a monthly subscription rate of 9000, and monthly "viewer/share" rate of 90,000. They offer display rates, as well as classified rates such as 8 rows of 32 characters for $125 for 2 months. To ask about other rates, contact ads@prisonlegalnews.org.

How to Get Rich Selling Non-Nude Photos!

Selling non-nude photos to inmates is extremely lucrative, and the costs to get started are minimal!

For those of you who don't know, most prisons no longer allow nudity. Especially "frontal" nudity. Pictures or magazines of nice looking nude women are a hot commodity among prisoners, and since they cannot have them any longer, some crafty entrepreneurs have started selling the next best thing -- photos of women as scantily clad as possible while still being considered non-nude. Back shots of women in thongs; front shots of women in thongs, topless but nipples covered, etc. Usually the women are in the sexiest of poses and positions; as long as the pic doesn't show nipple or vagina (some are even very borderline), the picture will usually get through.

Starting a company like this is very easy. While a few companies have elected to use exclusive models (some of the companies are ran by a single model herself), most compile a collection from various online sources -- websites, Facebooks, Twitters, Instagrams, etc., both famous and not, and store them on a thumbnail. There are tons of beautiful women out there trying to market themselves in such a way, so they post their pics online for all to see (free) in hopes of catching the

GET MONEY: Self-Educate, Get Rich & Enjoy Life, Vol. 1

right eye. And since prisoners have no access to the Internet, you can capitalize off this by selling prints of the girls! Most models don't know they can make money selling photo prints to inmates and get a nice buzz/fanbase and income that way. If you are a model, this is something you surely should do. And if you're not a model; like most businesses, where others are dropping the ball, you pick it up! You can help promote the model(s) in ways they're not doing themselves and make a bunch of money doing it!

Though it varies, the usual price is $1.00 per photo. 4"x6", usually. Some companies make customers purchase a minimum per order -- usually 10 or so -- and of course shipping is usually charged. And at only 25¢ or so per photo for you, that's a 300% profit! Not a bad gig for a job you can do from your home computer.

To get started, once you've compiled what images you're going to use, and I suggest you start with at least 50 or more different ones, you want to make a "catalog." A catalog is typically one 8.5"x11" sheet with one or two-inch images of your entire collection on it -- for example, 8 across and 10 down, or something. You will have to adjust the size depending on how many you are trying to fit on one side. You always want them big enough that inmates can see clearly enough to decide if there are any images they want to buy, but not big enough that inmates will be content when just having your catalog. You want to put an identifiable number or name under each photo so inmates can communicate which ones they want.

Some companies, especially when they are new, small, and trying to get a buzz of their own offer to give away their 1-page catalog(s) for free should the inmate send a SASE. Others may charge 3-4 stamps. It all depends on your costs -- whether you're printing at a professional printer in bulk or at home, whether they are color or black and white, whether it's printed on regular typing paper or glossy. Bigger companies, like Cold Crib and Prison Official sell their catalogs for $10 each. Their catalogs are 5.5"x8" booklets, maybe 30 pages, 500-1000 photos, full color and glossy. These companies make the inmate buy the $10 catalog, just to see if there are any photos they'd like to buy, then make the inmate buy a minimum order of 10 or so. There are a number of ways you can do this, but you get the point.

Once you have your product and your catalog, you need to get word out to as many inmates as possible that your company exists. There are several effective ways to do this. You can get a free text ad of 75 words or less in The BEST Resource Directory for Prisoners by emailing it to thecellblock.net@mail.com. To purchase bigger ad space, contact them for prices. The BEST Resource Directory for Prisoners is an inmate favorite. You can contact Diane, CEO of

41

Freebird Publishers, who publishes the Inmate Shopper, another directory-type book for prisoners at Diane@FreebirdPublishers.com about listing your company in her publication. You can advertise in Prison Legal News. They boast a subscription rate of 9,000 monthly subscribers, and a total "share" rate of 90,000. They offer advertising spaces for sale, including "classified" space with a rate of $125 for 2 months for 8 rows of 32 characters. Contact them at ads@prisonlegalnews.org. In addition to these places the more successful companies like Cold Crib and Prison Official advertise in the classifieds of men's magazines like Smooth, Black Men, and hip-hop magazines like XXL.

This is much more expensive to do. XXL charges $11.95 per word, 14 words minimum for classified rates (1 month), and $495.00 per column inch (2.25" w x 1" h) for display rates. I used to see Cold Crib and Prison Official each advertise 5-inch display ads in each issue. To have an advertising budget like this goes to show you just how much money these companies make! Like with any business, start slowly with whatever you can do. Wait for the money from that ad to come in and buy more ads at more places. Wait for that money to come in and expand again -- over and over until you have a large promo campaign going on and a dominate share of the market!

How to Start an Independent Record Label in 9 Steps!

A record label is basically a brand name connecting music to customers. Ideally, the label establishes a good enough reputation that when people see an artist or band signed to that particular label, they know it's going to be something they'll enjoy, and then buy the product without a second thought (and never regret it). If you want to start an independent record label, however, having good taste in music is not enough; you need to be a good businessperson.

Here are the steps you will need to take...

1. Think ahead. Although many successful record labels started off with someone winging it, there are many that fail for that very same reason: poor planning. Creating a record label is a business and a full-time job. Consider the following before you start one:

Cash flow. Do you have enough money to pay for manufacturing? What about promotional materials? It'll be a while before you get any money back from records selling (if they sell at all). You might need a grant or loan to hold you over. Some labels raise extra funds by putting on club nights or gigs. You can also try crowdfunding, like Kickstarter. It's recommended that you don't quit your day job.

Business plan. Independent record labels can take off without a business plan, but you'll need one eventually, so why not write one now, when it'll benefit your business the most? You'll definitely need one if you want to apply for grants or loans, and it's a good idea to have one if you ask people to invest in your business.

Licenses and forms. Think about how you want to structure your business: sole proprietorship? partnership? corporation? Get a business license and file appropriate tax forms. Register with any relevant organizations (e.g. Mechanical-Copyright Protection Society). You may also need a retail license if you're selling records directly to the public.

Note: If you decide to work with a partner or partners, ideally you will want to work with people you can rely on, trust, share and receive information with and most importantly people you can get along with. Working with friends is great but remember and remind them it has to be as professional and timely as possible, especially in the beginning stages because this is where a company can fall apart and end altogether. Having fun is always great for the job setting but there has to be a line in the sand which all parties cannot cross.

Office space. You can get by with just a post office box and a business phone number, or you can establish a complete office, if you have the funds. You can build your own studio or pay for studio time somewhere else.

2. Choose a name. Brainstorm 5-10 good names that you feel will fit your business. You need to tell people who you are and the type of music you produce. In short, your business name should say it all. The reason for choosing a number of names for your record label is that if one is taken you can still fall back on the others and not have to waste time rethinking your names.

Go to a domain name registry and see if any of these names are already taken. Try for .com and .net as these are the most popular and visitors will be familiar with them. The quick check will tell you if anyone has the names already online and will help you with your ultimate choice.

Consult local government (the State Registrar in the US) to check if any offline businesses have these names. This will ensure that you are the sole user, and nobody can infringe on your rights. It also stops you from any unpleasant lawsuits later on if people contend your rights to use a business name.

Select one unique name. Choose the best name from among the ones that you are left with. Remember it needs to be one that is appropriate for your business and music. Register a domain name for your upcoming website. It is important to do this quickly before it gets taken by someone else. When you register your domain name, always get both .com and .net so that nobody can have a similar name to you and leech off your marketing efforts.

Register the name with the appropriate authorities. This will make sure that this is exclusively your own business name and will protect your rights. You may need to file a DBA (doing business as) license so you can identify with your label's name when conducting business (accepting and making payments, for example).

Design a logo. You might also want to print stickers, posters, stationary, business cards, etc.

3. Corner your market. Choose and study your genre. Sit down, either alone or with your partner(s) and think of the style(s) you want your record label to be. It would be best if you picked a style that you are very familiar with and have extensive knowledge about. Musicians don't like being forced into a box but choosing and sticking with a particular genre helps a record label know their market (who buys that genre) and build contacts with people who deal with that genre (record shop owners, DJs, journalists etc.). Research your genre and find out what it's missing. Observe and predict trends. You need to fill a niche. Talk to local promoters, studio owners, music shows, distributors, journalists, and anyone who can offer insight about what's hot and what's not. Who is your target audience? How old are they? What are they buying? This is also good research for a business plan.

4. Find talent. Scour the local band scene and find bands who you think will earn your label a good reputation in your genre. You can't compete with the big record labels, so you want to go for interesting records that slip under the radar but will be a hit with your specific market. After you find a band or artist you feel is a great fit for your label, talk with the band, artist, or their manager and offer a contract signing them to your label. The key word here is "sign." That means you should have a contract for every artist, drawn up by a qualified lawyer. If a track or an artist gets big and you don't have a contract, things can turn ugly, and your label might get the short end of the stick. Some labels don't do contracts if there are one or two singles at stake but insist on contracts when there's an album deal on the table.

5. Record in a studio. If the artist doesn't have a recording and you don't have a studio, shop around. Look for an engineer who has experience in your genre and an owner you can work with. You might be paying for some or all of the studio

GET MONEY: Self-Educate, Get Rich & Enjoy Life, Vol. 1

time. Ask about lower rates if you block book time for two or three projects. It's a good idea to have a producer there (you or a musician you trust) to make sure everything turns out well (and your money isn't wasted). It can cost $75+/hour. If you pay for a portion or all of the recording, then you can withhold earning from the band/artist until you make back all the money you put into the recording, and you have more of a say in how the album sounds. This needs to go in the contract, though.

6. Promote the music. Your goal here is to do everything you can to chart locally. Make enough copies of the music to promote it as follows:

Contact local college radio stations -- push to get your music played.
Send recordings to independent magazines and newspapers -- hope for favorable reviews.
Put on great performances. The members of the audience will go home and tell their friends about your fabulous show.

Print your website address on the program so that you can attract your fans to the website and they will buy more.

Sell copies at the show. Make notes of the songs that your live audience love and record them into a DVD or album of your greatest hits.
Sell them from your website and allow a sample to be downloaded from your site.

Make use of social media to promote the music on a larger scale.

Give away free tickets to your upcoming show/concert.

You can even pitch the music for televisions shows, commercials, cell phones, and video games, but get legal advice before licensing the music.

7. Press the product. Get the records mastered before sending them to a manufacturer, if necessary. Ask around. Get quotes. The more copies you make, the lower the cost per copy. When choosing packaging, think about how retailers will display them. Ask distributors for advice.

In the US, each release will need a catalog number (usually a 3-letter abbreviation followed by the numbers, i.e. CJK415) and a universal product code (the bar code on the back of the product) to be seriously considered by distributors.

8. Sell the music to distributors. To get as much product on retail shelves as possible, you need to convince distributors to help.

They will want to see that you've established some success on your own (charting locally, selling product on consignment, live shows, mail order and other direct sales methods) before they even consider carrying your music. Here are some questions you will want to have answers for before you even contact a distributor:

Has the artist had any success with established mainstream labels?
Does the artist have a following, if so, how well known are they?
If the artist is unknown, what specific promotion ideas does the label have?
Are there any well-known "guest" musicians on the recording?
Does the recording and artwork meet the standards of the musical genre?
Is there any current airplay on commercial or non-commercial radio?
Will there be independent promotion on the release to retail and to radio?
Has the artist hired a publicist, and/or what is the publicity campaign?
Will the artist be touring in support of their release, and is there a schedule?
Does the record label have the financial resources to provide "co-op" advertising, in which the record label and retailer split the cost of media ads?
Does the label have the financial resources to press additional product?
Does the label have a salable "back catalog" of proven sellers?
How much product from the label is already out in stores?
Does the label have other distributors selling the same product?
What are the next releases from the label, and when are they coming out?
How are sales/downloads of the artist's release doing on the Internet, and such sites as iTunes.com, cdbaby.com, and your social media platforms?

Product is sold to distributors for about 50% of the list price and is accepted on a negotiable billing schedule of 60-120 days per invoice. The label usually pays for shipping charges. Most national distributors require that they are the only distributor of a particular product. You might also be required to pay for advertising on the distributor's monthly newsletters, and/or update sheets, as well as catalogs (costs subtracted from invoice).

You'll also need to give them a negotiated number of free copies for promotional purposes, along with "Distributor One Sheets" (fact sheets with promotion and marketing plans and price information) and "P.O.P."s (Point of Purchase) items, like flyers, posters, cardboard standups, etc., for in-store display.

Distributor One Sheets should have the following information on a single sheet: label's logo and contact information, artist name/logo, catalog # and UPC code

(barcode), list price (i.e. $15.98) of each available format, release date (to radio), street date (for retailers, if different than release date), brief artist background description, selling points (discounts, marketing and promotion plans).
All promotional product needs to have the artwork punched, clipped, or "drilled" to make sure they aren't returned to the distributor as "cleans" (retail product).

9. Keep your fingers crossed. In the music industry, it's often hit or miss. Hopefully, the music will connect with your market and sales will take off, but some of your music, sooner or later, will bomb. Try to make it so the big successes cover your losses, with extra left over to pay for operating expenses (and your own paycheck, so you can keep doing what you love without starving).

Tips

If the artist has had success in a particular market already, you can send the recording to distributors before you send it to radio stations so that people can buy the records once they hear the music.
Some labels double as the artists' management.
As you get better known, you may start touring the country and even abroad. Just one or two albums can skyrocket you to success. However, never rest on your laurels as your competition is never far behind. It will not take them long to start butchering your work. Keep one step ahead of them by protecting your rights and finding new, unique talent. In this way, you will keep a hold on the market.

Warnings

Money is the biggest issue of any business so make sure you have figured out your money situation.

Be prepared for long hours.

Always set money aside for marketing and promotion.

Seven Secrets of Book Selling Success!

Dozens of men and women across the nation have become wealthy in the booming book sell-ing business. Hundreds more have been very successful. Yet, thousands have managed to enter and leave the business after having spent more than they earned. Why? Is book selling success an elite club? Do you need to know the "right" people to get somewhere in the industry? Or, is it just that those who've "made it" have simply done more things right and fewer things wrong?

After conducting a lengthy investigation of the super book selling successes, I can conclude that there are a few secrets anyone wishing to be a success must learn. Seven to be exact.

And, whether they will admit it or not, all the mail order "heavies" have used all seven religiously…in every single successful promotion. Those who have enjoyed a degree of success have used at least five of the seven secrets in their successful promotions. And, those who have failed dismally generally used four or fewer of these secrets in their book selling efforts.

In short, in the book selling business it's what you know, not who you know that counts. What's incredible is that so many people have plunged into this business without assuming that at least a few tricks-of-the-trade were involved. Consider that if it takes up to ten years to become a doctor, seven to be a lawyer, and several years of technical training to run a printing press, how does any-one leap to the conclusion that all there really is to mail order selling is placing ads, stuffing envelopes, and licking stamps? Mail order book selling, like any other business, is a skill to be learned.

Any business is based on sound planning. Sales result from a careful study of the market, a con-sideration of customer wants and needs, and the meeting of those needs and desires. The mail order book selling business is no exception. Each of these factors is taken into consideration and neatly incorporated into the seven secrets. If you publish or sell books to mail order buyers, you must con-sider these seven secrets.

Here they are:

1. EVERY BOOK MUST FIND TWO NEEDS AND FILL THEM

The adage that says you must find a need and fill it will not by itself satisfy the book buying mar-ket. If you want to sell a lot of books, you must capitalize on multiple appeals. One of those appeals should almost always be "how to earn more money". This is because, with non-fiction books, extra cash is as close to a universal appeal as there is. Money can be tied to almost any other appeal—from bass fishing to matchbook collecting. This idea should permeate the entire book. It can be spelled out in the book title and carried throughout the book.
The second appeal must fill a genuine need. As good as the "extra money" need is, it will seldom pull well enough by itself to sell the volume of books you'll

require. It's just too general. People are naturally suspicious of non-specific offers. You need a second, specific appeal. It must fill a need that is sufficiently limited to be covered in a single book. And the book content must fulfill this second need. It should convey enough useful information to convince the buyer that the book was worth the purchase price.

If a book does these two things: Promise to fill two needs (the desire for extra income and one more), and then actually fill them with worthwhile information, then your book has met this important first criterion. Whether the book requires 10 pages or 10,000 to do this is relatively unimportant. Yet, if it fails in either area, a million pages won't make it any easier to sell.

2. THERE MUST BE A WIDESPREAD DEMAND

The saintly little old lady with the tremendous idea of writing a book about "Crochet Needle Collecting" was shocked when an editor suggested that perhaps only five copies could be sold in the entire nation. The book would have been beautiful. After all, she had the most complete and elabo-rate collection of hooks in the world...and she was the planet's most knowledgeable expert in the field. The colorful language and delicate photographs would have produced a book that anyone would judge to be a work of art. But, who would buy it?

You need a big market. The bigger, the better. That doesn't mean you must avoid books that are too general. It means that the potential market should not be overly limited, as in the example above. If everyone except the very rich or the "already professional" in the area the book deals with would find it appealing, you have a winner.

As with most of the books, there is no question as to their widespread interest-producing nature. When in doubt, however, try a poll. Ask 100 people point-blank:

"I'm not selling anything today but would be interested in your opinion. Would you consider buying a book, any book, by mail? Would you consider buying a book of interest without ever having seen it, if it were returnable with a money-back guarantee? Would you consider buying a book about (your topic) by mail under the above conditions?

Eliminate those who would not consider buying a book by mail from your calculations. Zero in on potential buyers, and note the number who claim that they would, or might, consider a book on your topic. If more than 30% say "yes" or "maybe", you may have a winner. If more than 60% say "yes" or "maybe", you know you have a winner. And, if more than 90% give you the nod, pull out all the stops and launch your ad campaign immediately!

A book with a mass market will sell itself. A book without one should never have been written in the first place. If you happen to enjoy a rather obscure and unique hobby, keep it obscure. Never let that personal interest affect your selection of books to sell. The bigger the pie, the bigger your slice. Remember that.

3. ADVERTISE CREDIBLY AND EMPATHETICALLY

The old commercials promising to "kill germs on contact" and demanding on the product label that you "accept no substitutes" represent the kind of ads we used to get away with.

Today, however people probably would not be swayed by such an ad. A demand that no substitutes be accepted is a concept with which the consumer can no longer identify. Today, advertising appeals must directly appeal to a potential benefit for the consumer.

People must believe your ad if you are going to sell a lot of books. If your ad can't be trusted, how can the reader hope to rely on the information in your forthcoming book? Old ads that made false claims have sown seeds of disbelief that are being harvested today in a bumper crop of cynicism. Your ads must counter this reaction with human appeal.

Ads should contain at least one disclaimer—one admission that at least a part of your book is not going to work miracles overnight. One or two such admissions, honest but not damaging, can work wonders in making your offer seem genuine. Everyone knows that nothing that's genuine is perfect. So, take your book off its pedestal by admitting that it won't replace the Bible, but it can provide spe-cific benefits that are next to irresistible.

Follow these guidelines. Prepare your ad truthfully and with a benefit-oriented appeal. Then, set your ad aside for a day. Think about something else, anything else during that time. Then, come back to your ad. Read it objectively. Decide if it measures up. If it's still an appeal to which you would per-sonally respond...run it. It will sell books.

4. PRICE ACCURATELY AND PROFITABLY

Information on single sheets of paper has sold for thousands of dollars in years past. And it still does. By contrast, hundreds of newspaper pages in Sunday editions—some in full color—have also sold for as little as a quarter. Your responsibility is relatively simple. Find the most profitable selling price for the book you offer.

Doing this requires testing (as you'll see in Secret Six). What you want is both the price that pro-duces the highest profit and the one which produces the greatest number of customers—in that order. For example: If a book priced at $20, $15, $10, and $5 produces these results in four different price tests, which price will you select?

	A	B	C	D
Selling Price	$20	$15	$10	$5
Number of Sales	300	550	800	1200
Gross Profit	$600	$8250	$8,000	$6,000

The $15 price tag has clearly produced the most dollars. It is the most profitable price. Once the cost of the book (which will be the same regardless of what it sells for) is subtracted from the gross sales figure, the $15 price will appear even more appealing. If your purpose is a one-time-only sale (which it should seldom be, if ever), then the $15 price is the one to use.

But, see how close the $10 price tag comes in this example. It produces almost the same number of dollars of revenue, but 45% more customers! Not only will you earn far more in the long run (espe-cially by applying Secret Seven) but, the names of customers themselves can be sold or rented for additional income throughout the year.

Long-term profits represent the importance of testing price accurately. The results will vary from one market group and product to another, so remember to re-test when you enter a new market, rent a new list, or plan to advertise in a new magazine. The real test of profitability is not how much you make per book, but how much you make per advertising dollar spent. Approach pricing from this per-spective and you will always operate profitably while selling more books.

5. CLINCH SALES WITH A 100% MONEY-BACK GUARANTEE

A 100% guarantee has a single purpose: to remove any remaining barrier that might keep the reader from buying immediately. If a book is of reasonable quality, 98% of your buyers will keep it. And, by including bonus offers bound into the book itself which would be lost if the book were returned, you can increase so-called "customer satisfaction" to 100%.

Guarantees serve the purpose of keeping a customer from "losing face" later on when he or she suddenly feels "ripped off" by shoddy merchandise that was peddled at too a high price.

Often, when customers know they can return something, the psychological need to do so vanishes. Also, a sense of trust and credibility which the ad begins to build within the reader is reinforced by a strong guaran-tee of satisfaction or money back.

Standard guarantees run from seven days to as long as a year—or even a lifetime! Each is based on its own set of psychological principles and the nature of the product being offered. A thirty-day money-back guarantee is almost universal in the book business. This allows sufficient time for the reader not only to read and evaluate a given book, but also to forget it.

People's interests are usually cyclical. The strong immediate interest at ordering time wanes until it is rekindled by the arrival of the book itself. Then, there is sustained interest through the first reading of the book. In this phase, the book should deliver on enough of its promises for the reader to decide that "this material is valuable enough to keep on hand. I want to re-read it again as soon as I have a chance." That re-reading will usually not occur until thirty to sixty days later. By that time, any thoughts of returning it have expired...right along with the guarantee.

Conversely, a seven-day guarantee can actually apply enough psychological "pressure" to force a hurried evaluation "in time to beat the guarantee deadline". This can actually stimulate an artificial number of returns.

So, use guarantees properly. Understand in advance that their purpose is to encourage sales while allowing thoughts of return to die a natural death of complacency. Your guarantee should allow the buyer to think, "Oh, why not, I can always return it if it turns out to be a lemon," and, "Well, I've got plenty of time to read it again before sending it back". In the mind of the book owner after the first reading...your sales success is, of course, GUARANTEED!

6. STRUCTURE A TEST WITH "ROLLOUT" POTENTIAL

If you've read any good book in the mail order field, you've undoubtedly encountered the test stress! TEST! TEST! TEST! That's just wonderful. But, why? To keep from losing a lot of money on a nothing ad, a ho-hum list, or a dead magazine audience? Maybe it's to find out if blue colored ink pulls better on puce or purple paper? Well, all these things may simulate a test. But, if there are any iron-clad rules in the industry, they are these.

Test Only Primaries. Test only the ad, offer, list, magazine, or the price. Leave paper shade and forward or reverse paper fold tests to the mail order sophisticates who get paid for coming up with new variables to test.
Test Only When a Roll-Out Potential Exists. Never test too small a list. If a given list has 10,000 names and a valid test involves 5,000 of them (which is a general rule, regardless of list size), then even if it's a super puller, the expensive test results aren't going to go very far.
There are only enough names left for another reasonable test. However, a list with 100,000 prospective names deserves a test of 5,000. If the initial mailing pulls well, you can make a killing on the other 95,000 names. Right?

So, when the situation warrants it, test ad copy price, offer, list, or magazine. If conditions don't warrant a test—perhaps the list or readership is too small—don't use it at all. Find a bigger target—one with rollout potential. After all, that's the whole purpose of testing, isn't it?

To duplicate a small-scale success on a large scale while cutting small scale losses short is the stuff of which testing is made!

7. DESIGN A BUILT-IN FOLLOW-UP PROMOTION

Success begets success. It's supposed to happen. Why not "make it happen"? It's easy with a little advanced planning. And, it's the big secret of many mail order millionaires. One common approach is to keep an accurate record of all book buyers by title, then offer them a book in a similar interest area a few weeks later. This is effective. But, there's an even better way. Build the "tag-offer" or "back-end promotion" right into the book itself. Make it a part of the book.
There are two basic approaches to this method:

Offer an item of related interest. With books, offer a second book in the same subject category with a different or supplementary content.

Offer a book or item that is an integral part of the first book. For example, an ad in a book on brain surgery could contain an ad on the last page for a genuine stainless-steel scalpel for just $4.98. Get the point? As interesting as the subject matter may be, the reader cannot begin to actually perform cranial surgery on his mother-in-law or sister without taking advantage of the scalpel offer.

When possible, this second approach always outpolls the first one. However, both approaches make additional sales, producing additional revenue without the expenditure of a dime of additional advertising cost. The built-in ad becomes part of the "literature" of the original book. It adds a page of thickness to the manuscript, hence, additional value to the reader who values his or her library by its weight. And additional pages look good when mentioned in the book's original ad. Most importantly, it adds more dollars to your pocket without extra effort.

A well-structured in-text promotion can double or triple profits from a particular offer. If, after the dust settles, a $10 book has cleared $2 per book after paying for the book, the ad, and the postage; an in-test promotion that produces an average of $3 more per book is all gravy. It increases total prof-its by 150%!

Another key element in built-in promotions is that they have an incredible life. Newspaper ads gen-erally have a life of one week, maximum. Monthly magazines pull for three to as long as 18 months after publication. But books pull for years. If properly structured they can elicit responses from several different owners, plus scores of readers of a single copy. If the price structure of your in-text offer is one that can stand the test of time, it will pay you for a long time to come.

Put built-in promotions into the books you write. If you don't have the time to write in text ads your-self, use the camera-ready originals that are provided by the original publishers. And if you don't, make sure you keep accurate records of who buys what. Even though follow-up promotions are a lit-tle more expensive due to printing and mailing a follow-up circular or letter, they're a lot less expen-sive and more productive than finding a brand-new customer. Well-designed follow-up promotions can bring you business for a lifetime.

Those are seven secrets that can change your chances of mail order success. You can take a mediocre text and turn it into a hot-selling winner if you carefully plan your book. Proper develop-ment, advertising, testing, and follow-up can tip the scales in your favor. Why not give it a try? You have nothing to lose and everything to gain.

How to Get Rich Publishing Material You Get FREE!

Basic Starting Point: The Concept... In the USA, all government publications are not copyrighted. That means that any government publication can be freely copied. If all publications of the USA government were placed end to end, they would be a paper carpet to the moon and back. All subjects imaginable are covered by books funded and published by the US government. If you look at a list of topics most favored by readers around the world, there are at least a thousand government publications on each one of those subjects! Be it gardening, dog training, speaking Swahili, raising babies or surviving in a jungle, there is a government publication about it! The US government has informative publications on every aspect of every obscure country around the world. Government books contain hundreds of pages of maps and photos on the most obscure places.

Government publications are prepared at great expense (up to several million dollars of taxpayers' money funding the research on each book), and make for very interesting reading. Some are pretty boring with narrow focus on subjects you can't believe anyone would be interested in. From time to time you will hear that thousands of pages of expensive research has gone into a study of Eskimo ear wax or something equally obscure. Another aspect to bear in mind is that similar grants might be available to you to write for the government. They have many "make work" programs for artists, writers, film makers, composers, poets, and almost everyone else. But that is not the main idea I want to share with you about government publications.

The idea here is to find a government publication of general interest and to market it as your own product. Example? There are manuals prepared for soldiers, sailors and marines on every subject from training watch-dogs and making biological weapons to identifying badges of rank and medals in other military services. The military instruction manuals also deal with many non-military subjects, such a food preparation for large and small groups, or leading exercise classes. All of these books and pamphlets are in public domain. Public domain means anyone can copy them and with or without editing, publish them at any price they choose.

Some government publications are given away free, but others bear price tags that sometimes seem much more expensive than a private bookseller would charge for a similar book. Do you smell opportunity? If you don't, you are not thinking like a true hustler. Marketed correctly, government publications, with or without new material, can legally be sold at any price the "packager" of this material chooses to set. Do other governments allow private citizens to pick and choose and republish such information? Some do, and some don't. But all material of a certain age, usually 50 years, is in the public domain because copyrights are only for limited periods. Thus, you don't have to pay anyone to put out a volume of Shakespeare's sonnets, portions of the bible or recordings of jazz hits from the 1930s, etc.

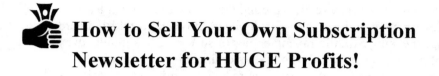 How to Sell Your Own Subscription Newsletter for HUGE Profits!

The explosive growth of desktop publishing has made it easier to write and publish your own material. If you have special knowledge in a particular field about which others would enjoy reading, you could easily begin your own subscription newsletter. With a little time and effort, you could develop it into a widely-distributed publication -- and make lots of money in the process!

Newsletter publishing appeals to many different people because of its relative simplicity and minimal initial investment. Yet, it can be highly profitable. According to one recent report, newsletters produce an estimated two billion dollars in revenue annually! Although composed of few pages, newsletter subscriptions can run upwards of $100 annually. You can see how easy it is to make a handsome profit!

If you publish an eight-page newsletter with an $80 subscription price and you sell only 1,000 subscriptions, you will take in $80,000. Even if your overhead is 50%, you will still realize a profit of $40,000. And even if you have to write all the articles yourself, it would still be a part-time job at best. Yes, newsletter publishing can be very profitable!

To choose a topic about which to develop a newsletter, take a look at yourself and your interests. What areas appeal to you? Do you have a particular hobby? What types of books do you like to read? What do you do in your spare time? Most likely you will discover that you can turn your interest or hobby into a profitable newsletter. One guy I know took an interest in history and developed a monthly newsletter featuring new studies in the field. He eventually sold the operation to another dealer for quite a profit. You could do the same with computers, book collecting, art, prison topics, or any other topic. Turn your interests into income!

If you own a personal computer, your task will be greatly simplified. Any number of word processing programs, for either IBM compatibles or Apple Macintosh, will allow you to design and lay out a newsletter. Many programs have several built-in newsletter templates. All you have to do is insert the graphics and text.

An eye-catching design win help you will more subscriptions. But, if you do not have a computer, you can still develop a winning newsletter. Simply type up your articles in a clean, easy-to-read format. Use paste-up clip art to highlight sections and break up large blocks of text.

Take a look at several of the more widely circulated newsletters already on the market. They have likely been designed by professionals. Copy the design elements that appeal to you. You may also want to look at books that address typography and design. As you study, you will gain new insights into what factors will help your newsletter succeed. You'll pick up a few basic pointers that will help you create a winning, attractive newsletter.

Once you have prepared the basic design of your publication and are gathering information for the first issue, begin your promotion campaign. If you regularly read large, national magazines in a field of interest like the topic of your newsletter, place one or more classified ad in them offering a free or low-cost sample issue of your newsletter. When folks respond, send the sample issue along with a sales letter and subscription offer. Some will write simply to get something free. However, if you have advertised in a magazine whose readers are strongly interested in your topic, you will gain a large number of subscriptions. You will also want to create a direct mail campaign aimed at potential subscribers. You can rent a mailing list of subscribers to the national magazines in your field. In the beginning, when funds are low, you will want to mail to a small number. Since most mailing list brokers require that you rent a minimum of 5,000 names, start there. Always mail by third class bulk rate to keep costs low.

If your first mailing goes out to 5,000 people and you have a 5% response, you will gain 250 new subscribers. If each pays the $80 subscription price, that's $20,000 -- enough to pay the cost of printing and mailing your offer to all 5,000 potential subscribers, filling the 250 subscriptions for one year, and still leave you a tidy profit. Roll your profits over and invest in a larger mailing list -- and just repeat the process for an even greater payoff!

Testing has shown that your mail solicitation should include five basic elements:

Outer envelope with teaser copy.
One or two-page sales letter.
Small fold-over note to emphasize the offer.
A reply card.
A post-paid reply envelope.

The Cell Block Presents TCB University

Your outer envelope should be imprinted with some sort of teaser copy that will prompt the recipient to open it and investigate. If you can't capture his attention when he first sees the piece, he is more likely to simply throw it in the trash unopened than to investigate further. If possible, print the teaser in a colored ink that will also call attention to your offer.

Your sales letter must directly offer benefits to the potential subscriber. He must be convinced that there is "something in it for him." Whether your newsletter offers to make the reader wealthier, happier, slimmer, smarter, a better cook -- whatever -- you must stress the direct benefits of the product to the reader. Tell him what you're offering, why he should subscribe, what he can expect in return, how he can profit, what guarantee you offer, etc. If possible, offer an additional "free" bonus along with his subscription. This offer will sway the undecided. It will cost you little but will make all the difference in the world.

The small fold-over note is simply a short, second sales letter. Often, the outside is printed with a slogan like, "Only open this if you've decided NOT to subscribe" or something similar. It also must capture the reader's attention, giving you a second chance to address any objections the reader might have, breaking down his sales resistance. It is best printed on a colored paper.

The reply card allows the new subscriber to fill in the pertinent information ---name, address, method of payment, etc. It also allows you to reiterate your guarantee and the personal benefits the subscriber will receive. The post-paid reply envelope (usually a Business Reply Envelope) allows him to return the card free of charge. It means a small cost to you but is well worth the expense of gaining a new customer.

What type of information will you include in your publication? Your newsletter may summarize information taken from other sources, such as magazines or books. You cannot copy other people's articles word for word, but you can rewrite the information and use it in your own articles. If this is your aim, stress to the subscribers that you will save them time by sifting out the important news from all the other "fluff" they generally have to plow through in order to find out what they need to know. You can gather stories for your newsletter from many sources. You can summarize articles from professional journals or from the national wire services. But, be careful not to violate the copyright laws when doing so.

One of the best sources for news -- in almost any field -- is the so-called information Superhighway, known as the Internet. You can "subscribe" to E-mail groups whose members daily write back and forth to one another discussing developments in their fields of interest. This data can be summarized and expanded into long and short articles for your newsletter. Many of these letters can be printed directly into your newsletter with no editing needed. Although the data is technically public domain, you could ask the author's permission to publish it by sending him or her an E-mail message. Best of all, the information often comes from the world's leading experts in the field, making your newsletter a top-quality publication!

If your newsletter is widely read, you may be sent query letters by potential writers suggesting future stories they would like to write. While it may at first glance appear expensive to pay for stories, it is really not. Most publications pay only five to ten cents a word for stories. Some pay a flat fee. If the story looks good and you can negotiate an agreeable price, go for it!

Here is a partial listing of some of the types of newsletters that are being published today.

Internet Tips
Inside Professional Sports News
Investment Advice
UFO Sightings
Soap Opera News
Book Reviews
College Fraternity News
Antique News
Inside Hollywood Gossip
Bookseller News
Prison Legal News
Aspiring Writer's Tips
Hip Hop News
Free Items
Computer User Tips
Mail Order Sales Tips
Food News
Sorority News

I hope I've sparked your interest in newsletter publishing. You can make a great profit if you develop a winning publication. All it takes is a little study, determination, careful consideration of the potential market, and the development of a unique method to meet the needs of potential subscribers. I wish you every success in your endeavor.

How to Get Rich Selling Information!

Wealth! The single greatest focal point of power, influence, and control in the world. It arrests attention, commands respect, and dictates loyalty. You are a person who wants great wealth and all the power and prestige that accompany it. And, you can have it. You can follow the same path that many others have walked to develop your own wealth through information marketing.

From the moment, you learn how to achieve wealth, you will have become instantly successful. The power and control you seek will already be yours. Others will recognize that you possess a secret. They will realize that you possess the knowledge of wealth. And, they can make you even wealthier.

This appetite for wealth is possessed by nearly everyone. Yet, many wish for it in a hopeful, but helpless fashion. Others seek it in a blind, undisciplined, headlong lunge toward opportunity. Still others make their quest an all-consuming passion; a driving, unrelenting desire that will overcome any obstacle to achieve the power and the glory that this goal promises.

Whatever your purpose and approach to wealth, you can learn the secrets of prosperity—secrets possessed by some of the world's wealthiest and most successful people. And you can make your dreams a reality.

Developing The Right Attitude Toward Wealth

A series of steps will take you to these heights of personal achievement and self-realization. Everyone, regardless of their degree of personal commitment to this goal, should take the first steps toward more complete fulfillment and accomplishment. And, because you possess a greater degree of commitment than most of those around you, there is nothing to prevent you from taking all of the steps in rapid succession...to become a focus of financial power.

The experiences that lead to power and wealth are not difficult to discover and unleash within yourself. You will quickly learn that they are all available by taking measured steps toward acquiring the necessary attitudes and techniques that produce greatness. By developing your own information marketing plan, you will be able to work toward your objectives.

Your attitude toward ventures and investments should change right now. You may have grown up in a society where the words "risk" and "loss" are almost a synonym for any kind of business or investment opportunity. This is the philosophy of the masses...not of the financial elite.

Risk is nowhere to be found in the vocabulary of the super-rich. The pretense of loss and financial hardship is faced, certainly. But, those with monetary wisdom rarely—if ever—assume risks of any size. They don't have to. With sufficient control over relevant circumstances, every investment becomes a "win-win" situation.

If those with vast wealth take such care, you can afford to do no less. If you do not have effective control of the investments, you now own (or direct inside information from those who do) you shouldn't be investing. If you don't have a comprehensive knowledge of the area in which you are investing—with a plan and specific goals based upon that knowledge—again, you shouldn't be investing.

Paul Getty admitted that all his dabbling on Wall Street was in oil stocks—his single area of unquestioned and perhaps unequaled expertise. He never played some other kind of stock for variety or sport. He invested knowledgeably with a plan. And, he made more in his stock market sideline by following this simple rule of investing knowledgeably than most people earn in a lifetime.

When Andrew Carnegie decided to enter the steel industry, he accumulated all the information he could find on steel and hired the most knowledgeable men in the world to establish and run what was to become his empire. To Charles Schwab, his key figure, he paid what was then the highest salary and bonus in the world.

Another important parallel can be drawn between these two examples. These men insured their success through cross-benefits and multi-profits. Their investments did more than produce a profit on their own. They simultaneously contributed to the interwoven success of other investments, providing a reinforcing or "synergistic" effect that hoisted profits in all areas by the bootstraps. The chart below illustrates how the varied facets of your enterprise should intertwine. The business strategies you are going to read will be presented with each of these ideas in mind.

You may have encountered some of these opportunities before. Others will be completely new to you. But, each of them has the important characteristics we've discussed. And, each of them is worth your close consideration. Remember:

- Your time and funds are too valuable to be threatened by an investment or venture that involves risk. The super-rich don't take risks because they don't have to. Neither do you.

- The element of risk is removed from an investment situation through a complete understanding of the investment and control of the factors which influence it.

- The prudent investor further insures success and profit through cross-investment and multi-profitability. An investment that develops profits and benefits for interrelated businesses and interests not only assures greater security, but greater overall gain. Even the possibility of loss is eliminated.

Choosing The Right Road To Wealth — Information Marketing

If you were forced to choose any single enterprise to enable you to most easily reach your financial goals, it would without question be the "Information Marketing Business". This includes the sale of books, manuals, and reports. No other single business has so many interwoven, multi-faceted benefits. And, no other business can have such an uplifting influence on your climb beyond mere financial independence to financial supremacy. Consider just a few of these benefits:

- Your own circle of friends is likely to become your first, and best, retail customers. They will want to emulate your success. To do so, they will need to study and learn what you know. The books have to be bought from someone. Why not your information marketing firm? Several thousand-dollars' worth of books at a minimum of 50% profit to you will get you well started down the road to wealth.

- Book buyers are really book collectors, adding to their libraries for a lifetime. They continue to buy month after month. Developing a list of book buyers guarantees a steady income at a high level of profit and gives your new firm a solid financial base.

- When you enter the publishing business and begin offering your own works (which you will want to do soon), this established market will produce a guaranteed level of initial sales, thereby taking the risk out of self-publishing.

- You are already a book buyer. From this moment, however, an important change has taken place. In addition to being a book buyer, you must also become a bookseller. And, as such, you now have the option of reading just about anything in print—free. You buy what you want at below wholesale, read it, study it, and then offer it to customers at retail. The books you read actually turn a profit for you.

- This opportunity for free self-education goes much further, however. You can become a world authority in a highly-specialized field, a connoisseur of the arts, a consultant offering expertise for business and industry, a sought-after author or lecturer, etc. And, the compensation for this type of knowledge in the form of gifts, honorariums, appointments, public offices, stock options, and more, can be considerable.

Establishing an information marketing firm requires little effort. Your city clerk can explain any local and state registration requirements. And, the fees, if any, are minimal.

The only important requirements are:

- A source of salable books at wholesale prices.

- A source of customers that match the kinds of books you wish to offer.

However, to build a business successfully in a short time with maximum profit, you must limit the scope of your book offerings to the most risk-free, high-popularity area and concentrate on building that market nationwide. And this area is how-to and self-help publishing. Books, reports, and manuals—like the one you are reading now—can make you wealthy. Publications that offer the reader a helping hand in helping themselves are always popular—among the best-selling books in the world!

Naturally, nationwide sales potential means mail order, not bookstore type of distribution. Nearly all self-published millionaire authors agree that no other sales method can compete with mail order marketing for the greatest profits, the widest exposure, the lowest operating cost, and the largest possible sales potential.

As a double bonus, mail-order book, tape, and educational material distribution receives preferential treatment and a preferential rate from the U.S. Postal Service under the special fourth-class rate. Not even first-class mail is designated as "special". But, your book shipments will be.

The Profit-Potential of Information Marketing

This field is the highest profit-maker in the mail order industry. That's why it is suggested as a no-contest first choice for making you wealthy. With as few as 20 good titles, all written by other authors, or with 2 or 3 titles of your own authorship, you can expect to earn an amount per year equal to your present annual income...but only working just a few hours per week. As your experience and the number of titles you offer increases, you can hope to exceed this amount by a large margin.

Remember, a large number of people fail in the mail order book business even though the odds of failure are far less than with any other kind of mail order company. The reason for failure is lack of knowledge...specifically a lack of understanding of the vital principles that you are learning with this report. These principles are the needs to:

- Eliminate Risk!
- Choose a Multi-Profit area!
- Become an expert in the business area you have chosen!
- Conserve your capital for advertising, not inventory!
- Create your own personalized ads and brochures from camera-ready materials!
- Buy books after they've already sold...at the best discounts!

The World's Greatest Information Marketing Method!

There is not sufficient room here to discuss all the possible methods of marketing information in detail. If you're in the right place at the right time, you may not need an elaborate method. Youn Mie Chellel of Hollywood just stands on the street corner at La Ciene and Sunset Boulevard and hawks his "Memory Maps", a self-published directory to the final resting place of the movie-world's greatest stars. He distributes them by hand, one at a time, $5 per map. If he seems to be doing it the hard way, it's worth noting that he earned more than $100,000 in his first three months!

There is, however, what most experts agree to be a best method. Here are the individual techniques of mail order marketing that can be applied to your sales plan. We've summarized each for you. While you will want to study each step in-depth, this synopsis will give you the general idea of how each operates and how it can benefit you.

The "Classified inquiry/Direct Mail Follow-Up" Technique

For just a few dollars, you can place classified ads for your books in front of tens of millions of readers. The idea is not to sell directly from the ad, however. Effective classifieds tell only enough to whet the reader's appetite for more. This appetite can be satisfied by sending for "Free Details". These interested people, or "inquirers", are immediately sent your sales literature—catalogs, brochures, etc. It is this package of material that will convince your inquirers to part with their money and purchase the book or books you're offering.

The "Multi-Mailing" Technique

What really makes this system profitable is that you are far from finished after the first mailing. A second mailing of sales literature will produce about 60% to 70% of the initial mailing's response. Therefore, if 10 out of 100 ordered the first time, 5 or 6 out of the remaining 90 inquirers are likely to order the second time, and 2 or 3 the third time. Since most direct mailings are profitable with a return of 2% or more, several succeeding mailings will add greatly to your total profits.

The "Subsequent Offer" Technique

After you have successfully completed your first sales campaign, you're ready to offer a similar book in a second direct mail attack. You can mail to your original list of book buyers first—for greatest returns—and your list of previous inquirers (but non-buyers up to now) for a secondary response. And, of course, continual classified advertising will allow your total list to grow larger constantly.

The "Mailing List Income" Technique

When the size of your list reaches several thousand names, it can be rented to other mail order marketers for $45 to $100 per thousand names, depending upon the quality and category of your names. Many list owners earn a nice profit on their list every year.

The "Instant Market" Technique

Finally, as you begin writing and publishing your own books and reports, not only will you have an instant market for almost anything you write...but, profits will be two to three times greater because of the low cost of printing your own titles.

The "Built-In Catalog" Technique

Profits can be increased still further by using the last few pages of your book as a catalog. Inserting a one-page ad for another of your titles in the back of your self-published book could significantly increase your earnings.

In summary, remember that books are the ultimate product, and book buyers the ultimate customers. Capitalizing on these facts allows you to build the "ultimate business". Choose the information area with the highest volume and profit and the widest range of multi-profitability opportunities. In this way, every effort provides potential income from several sources, allowing your wealth to accumulate quickly.

Self-Publishing For Success

Once you have established a successful information marketing business, you will be ready to enter the world of self-publishing. Entering the two businesses in this order eliminates risk and creates a reinforcing multi-profit effect. In many respects, it is identical to the previous venture, and most of the same techniques apply. There are three important differences, however.

- The percentage of profit you will earn from self-published materials can be double or triple what you earn from selling books by other authors. Since you control what your books and reports contain, you can include brief ads for your previous titles in every new book you write, thus increasing your overall exposure and sales.

- An entirely new wholesale market is opened, allowing you to drastically cut your printing costs on account of volume, while selling several hundred copies at a time. A $10 book can be printed for as little as $1, sold in large lots for $3, and drop-shipped at wholesale for $5 to the customer who purchases it for $10. Twenty regular customers who purchase large lots of books can move thousands of copies of your book per month.

- The world of individual title promotion also opens up when you begin self-publishing. To be profitable, most books require a minimum 3-to-1 (300%) mark-up. That means that a $10 book must cost no more than $3.33 in quantity. This is sometimes possible when promoting someone else's books. But, it should always be possible with your own. Frequently, a profit-promotion ratio of 5-to-1 (500%) and even 10-to-1 (1000%) or more, can be achieved.

An Instant Course in Effective Writing

Entire libraries have been devoted to the art of writing English prose effectively. Another book on the subject is certainly unnecessary. However, there are a few simple guidelines that you can keep in mind as you write. These are guidelines that will help make your writing more readable, and more saleable.

Write like you talk - Avoid shifting into some awkward form when you begin touching pen to paper. If your writing reads as you sound—barring any glaring grammatical errors—your style should be both popular and understandable. Don't worry too much about prepositions at the end of sentences or dangling participles. Just get your point across conversationally. 'Be yourself' on paper.

Keep sentences short - Sentence length should average 17 words or less to be easily readable. Ten words or less per average sentence represents an easily- readable length.

Use punctuation freely - Notice the liberal use of ellipses, dashes, and parentheses throughout these pages. An English professor might go into convulsions over this kind of prosaic butchery, but I believe that it improves clarity while seeming to reduce sentence length.

Employ optical paragraphs - Write shorter paragraphs, indent for a new paragraph every six or seven lines. Your writing will appear easier to read. And, the page looks more inviting to the reader.

Organize your thoughts- Write in a concise, logical pattern. If before you start you will prepare a terse outline of what you want to say, thoughts will come out in their proper order. And, in nearly every case, saying as much as possible in as few words as possible is worth far more than page after page of fluff or filler.

Rewrite often - There is no such thing as good writing, only good re-writing. The major function of the revision process is to slice away the "watermelon rind" of unnecessary words, leaving only the sweet, juicy heart on the page.

Anyone who will follow these simple guidelines can write one bestseller after another. To help get the words and thoughts flowing, read something from your favorite author in the field you're writing about. If you're worried about spelling and grammar, don't be. It's relatively easy to find someone to proof read your final draft and make cosmetic changes. Then too, even the finest books contain an error here and there.

How To Find Bestselling Topics And Titles

Here is a secret I have never shared in any other book. And, in all the reading I've done, I've yet to find anyone else who has revealed it. This principle is an almost foolproof method for finding popular titles and topics to write about.

First, you must be willing to discover what appeals widely to book buyers. Then, write a book that provides that appeal. So many would-be authors lead frustrated lives because they do things in reverse...writing a book that they like, then trying to find a market for it. There is no substitute for resolving to write what your audience wants to read.

Second, you must go to the one source that can tell you what book buyers want. You could ask your book loving friends, the local librarian, or your old high school English teacher. But, any information you receive from these sources would be nothing more than guesses. You must remove all risk by writing only what you know in advance will sell and sell wildly. There is only one source of this information: A large-volume bookseller who sells books in the same way you will be marketing yours.

If you cannot get this information by asking for it, then pay for it. You need to know which titles and which authors are selling the most books in your topic area. And, you need to own these books. By comparing the elements common to each of them, you can easily determine what your book must contain to enjoy the same popularity.

Finally, use this information to write the best book in print on the subject you have chosen. In many cases, this is far easier than it sounds. Most important, choose an earth-shattering title. Take time with it. Make a long list of possible titles and edit them. Try to keep the title under seven words. If more words are essential, consider the use of a sub-title. Include as many enticing promises as you can in those few words. If your title would also make a smashing headline for the book's sales literature, you can be sure you've chosen a winner.

Once you've pounced on a super-subject and written it with conversational clarity, you're ready to give it a winning appearance. Here is the true role of the publisher—to package the book in an attention-getting, sales-producing wrapper. As you have already guessed, these are a few tricks that will produce a better-selling book. And, sales are the only thing that counts!

All that is left is to merge your own books with the line you currently offer through your information marketing company. Send a copy of your originals to all the book wholesalers who advertise in the success and opportunity magazines, along with a copy of your wholesale price list. If you've followed the above instructions and studied the marketplace in advance, you will become a best-selling author.

The Profit Potential of Publishing

Hundreds of self-published authors have become multi-millionaires offering their books by mail nationwide. In fact, there is actually a world market for your books in English. The United Kingdom, India, Australia, Canada, and Hong Kong are all prime markets you can reach through foreign book importers. Writer Mark Haroldsen sold over half-a-million of his Wealth Formula books at $10 each. Joe Karbo, Owen Bates, Lee Howard, Ron Playle, Jerry Ruchannan, Robert Collier, Edmund Shaftesbury, and many others have experienced equal success.

You can join their ranks. But remember, even a marginal success will expand your capital and place you in a position to take advantage of even more of the investment strategies that will allow you to continue to build your own financial empire.

The publishing business is a logical follow-up to an information marketing business that allows you to multiply yourself and your income very profitably. Carefully choose your topic and write your book to create readable, marketable books and reports. Target your literary efforts by identifying best-selling titles and topics. Finally, use the pattern of other successful self-publishers to map your own road to success. Their books and ads are brilliant examples of exactly what to do and how to do it...to reach your established goals. The future waits. Get going!

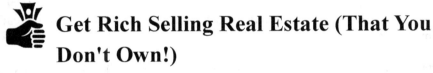 Get Rich Selling Real Estate (That You Don't Own!)

How can you "sell" something if you don't own or buy it first? What could be better than "controlling" real estate without buying that real estate? So, WHO makes money in real estate? The seller makes money. The real estate agent, bank, appraiser, lawyer, insurance agent, and even the city, county and state tax collectors make money. The BUYER pays something, even if he buys a distressed fixer-upper for no money down. His profits, which end up being the biggest of all, are deferred.

Each year poor slobs across this country who want to "Get Rich Quick in Real Estate" fall for the same old sucker-pitch. They buy courses, tapes, manuals and books on "How to Buy Distressed Properties," "Buy with No Money Down," "Buy Tax Lien Properties," "Buy Fixer-uppers."

In regular cycles of about ten years each, however, the markets become too crowded. It starts with everybody and their dog making money from ever-rising prices. Then all at once, the bubble bursts. Values often sink below the mortgage loan amount, and equity is wiped out. The financially strong or those who bought at the start of the boom hold on for an inevitable recovery. The weak hands are foreclosed upon. Those who bought cheap and are not highly leveraged can usually rent and hold on for a recovery –unless they made the mistake of buying in a bad location like say, Detroit. Real estate you buy must be in a great location where there are jobs, or other reasons for strong demand.

Real estate BUYERS have to make the monthly payments, pay the interest and principal, pay the taxes and assessments, and pay the cost of upkeep and maintenance. When they decide to sell they usually pay a six-percent commission to a local real estate agent. Of course, they can sell directly to a new buyer.

But here is a risk-free way to make money in real estate without investing anything:

You could become a real estate agent/broker and earn commissions for selling but being a real estate agent/broker requires a few courses and a license. It is a fulltime job that only pays well when the market is active and rising. It allows you to discover opportunities (bargain deals and partners) to build your own real estate empire, but it also requires a lot of work. There's nothing wrong with working, but here's the Lazy Man's Way to Riches in Property.

If you aren't a banker, appraiser, lawyer, insurance agent, or tax collector, and you want to be on the profitable selling side in real estate deals, consider using Real Estate Options. What is a real estate option?

A real estate option gives you control of a piece of real estate WITHOUT BUYING IT! By having an option on a piece of real estate property, you have the exclusive right to either buy that property, or NOT to buy it. The choice-option is yours. It is an "exclusive" right. That means that NO ONE ELSE can buy or sell that particular real estate property during the term of your option. It can be a lot, a house, a condo/apartment, a store, factory or warehouse. Any real estate.

During the period of your option, the owner keeps paying all of the inherent costs of the property such as taxes, assessments, upkeep and maintenance. He also collects the rent. In many cases, you as a tenant can get an option to purchase your own rental property from the owner. How?

You ask! "Mr. Landlord, your place is worth about $100,000. Would you give me the option to purchase it during my tenancy for $100,000 using any rent I have paid as the down payment?" As often as not, you will get an option. If you ask! In real estate, all such contracts must be in writing. But contract forms are usually free on the internet.

What could be better than "controlling" real estate without buying that real estate? Let the owner keep paying the taxes, maintenance and costs. During the option period, you can either sell the property, or sell the option itself, for a profit.

If the seller sells the property to someone else, while you hold this exclusive option, you are entitled to any monies the seller receives over the price you have agreed to pay for the property. Or, if the seller sells the property for less than what he agreed to sell it to you on your option, you are legally entitled to collect the difference from the seller.

"Exclusive" means "exclusive" under the law. When you hold an option on a real estate property, you "control" the sale of that property until your option expires. No one, not even the owner of the property, can buy or sell that property, legally, without first satisfying your option. You own the exclusive right to buy that property, or not buy that property, or sell that property to someone else, or sell the option itself to someone else.

When you use an option, you are NOT BUYING REAL ESTATE. You are buying the exclusive right to buy (or not buy) that real estate. That means you also have the exclusive right to sell the property as well.

Using an option, you also have another advantage. You will usually be dealing with "prime," or at least acceptable and presentable real estate properties. If you deal with "distressed" properties, you are often dealing with "garbage" real estate. Of course, at the right price, anything can be sold.

Suppose the apartment you occupy as a tenant needs some tender loving care (TLC) to make it shine and worth more than your option price? You fix it up, advertise, show it, and with any luck, you can make $50,000 profit on your option price of $100,000. If you don't get a buyer, assuming you have been paying, say, $1000 a month in rent for 2 years, you can go to a lender, show you have paid a $24,000 down payment in the form of rent, and get an 80% loan with payments similar or for less than the rent you have been paying. That's a no-money-down deal. When the smoke clears, you own your apartment and are paying less than you did to rent it.

It is easier to get a loan with evidence that you have been able to afford rent around the same as the future loan payments. Thus, you can use an option to buy an apartment you formerly rented. In this case, if the place is really worth $150,000, you have bought it for around half of value. The seller does not need a broker, and is probably going to be very happy to avoid the 6% broker's commission on a direct deal.

This is one way both insiders and novices can make money in real estate. It's done every day by people in the know. Like YOU!

 How a Teen Made Over $80,000!

At age 9, LeiLei Secor of Hagaman, New York, started making braided friendship bracelets. In her teen years, she branched out into beaded macramé jewelry. Then, as an incoming high school junior, she needed a summer job. "I couldn't find one," she says. "I thought, 'Why can't sell my jewelry online?'"

In July 2012, Secor opened a shop on Etsy.com, which allows artists to sell their products. Her shop, Designed by Lei, specializes in handmade wire rings and earrings. Just two years after the business launched, her profits are nearing six figures, which will help finance her college education.

Armed with self-taught techniques (Secor learned the art or wire jewelry-making on YouTube)

and a desire to set herself apart in an exceptionally competitive arena (in 2013, a million vendors sold goods on Etsy), she dived into research on photography, marketing and search engine optimization by comparing successful and unsuccessful Etsy shops, noting their different tactics. She uses a high-quality DSLR camera and natural light to achieve simple, elegant photography. Fans post the photos to sites such as Pinterest and Wanelo, generating a viral marketing buzz. As a result, Secor has sold more than 8,000 items, most priced around $10.

LeiLei's business has a clear marketing plan, incredible growth, a viral interest from potential customers and lots of additional upside potential.

Secor's jewelry-making and shipping supplies accompanied her to her dorm room at the University of Virginia, where she is studying business. She plans to invest around 12 hours a week in making jewelry and fulfilling orders, and after graduation, she hopes to work in finance or start another business.

"My Etsy shop has taught me not to shy away from any opportunity," Secor says. "It has made me fall in love with the entrepreneurial spirit."

10 Easy Ways to Build Your Social Media Following!

1. Have an excellent photo, bio, and profile. Every form of social media lets you provide some information about yourself. Make sure your profiles and bios include a succinct mix of who you are and what you do, but do not sell! Your photo should be a nice close-up of you alone -- preferably sporting a smile. Make sure the photo is clear and close; if it was taken from 50 feet away, you will look like a dot on a mobile device. And leave the photos of your family and friends to your Facebook photo album.

2. Cross-promote. Let people on Facebook have your Twitter handle, and people on Twitter find your Facebook page. Do the same on LinkedIn and other social media sites. A recent LinkedIn thread in a networking discussion group simple asked everyone to share their Twitter handles -- and they did.

3. Put your Twitter handle and Facebook page URL everywhere. Don't be shy about letting everyone know where you can be found on social media. Some folks even have bumper stickers with their Twitter handles on them. Are personalized license plates next?

4. Reciprocate. If they like you, like them; if they follow you, follow them; and if they endorse you, endorse them.

5. Be human. Use your own identity rather than your brand or logo. On Twitter, very often the people behind the business have more followers than their business. You can also link your business page on Facebook to your own webpage. Also connect with people behind other businesses; they can help you establish a relationship and you can even talk about, like, and cross-promote each other's companies.

6. Use photos. Yes, on Pinterest you will certainly be using photos. But they can be effective on your Facebook posts and your Twitter tweets as well. Photos grab people's attention. Make sure they are good quality and appropriate for your audience.

7. Pay attention. Each social media platform is trying to remain fresh, new and

innovative. As a result, there are new options introduced, some of which can benefit you in your effort to build your following and grow your brand. For example, in early 2013, Facebook came out with their new "Reply" feature, allowing you to respond immediately to other people's comments. You may not use the many features each social media platform has to offer, but it's worthwhile to stay abreast of the latest development.

8. Set up a schedule. While you may monitor social media all day long, you might be in a demanding job that doesn't let you spend great amounts of time actually being an active participant. If this is the case, you may want to set up a schedule to carve out time for making your presence felt.

9. Review what's working and what isn't. No matter what platform you are using, if growing a following and building your brand is your goal, you'll want to monitor your results. If you are putting yourself out there and people aren't responding, you may need to change your approach. If many people are liking your business on Facebook but ignoring you on Twitter, then focus on Facebook, or vice versa. Use tools such as Facebook Insights to find out where your "likes" are coming from.

10. Be interesting. I can't reiterate this enough: If you are interesting and engaging, people will engage with you; if you are boring, they won't. Choose your posts or tweets carefully.

Building a following will take some work; the good news is, you can do it from your office, your home, or while sitting on the beach with your trusty tablet. Remember to tweet -- or post -- often.

 ## How to Find Your Audience on Social Media

Before engaging on any platform, you need to determine who makes up your target audience. The overall marketplace is segmented with numerous niche markets and you need to identify yours. You can dig deeper than before when researching demographics today. You can use tools like Google Analytics to see exactly where visitors are coming from and how long they are staying on each page. You can determine what people are liking most on your Facebook page and compile some of your own audience demographics. If you're just starting out, you need to identify prospective clients with whom you will engage.

Platforms such as Facebook offers tools like "Insights" with interest graphs and social graphs that compile the interests of the user and the data from his or her friends. So, if a 24-year-old male has an interest in soccer and socializes with numerous other soccer enthusiasts, a sporting goods business might target him and his friends. As you seek out data, you can hone in on your region, city, or country. In some instances, you may even find that certain products are well liked in areas far from your location. One clothing retailer in Baltimore sells certain styles, colors, and brands of apparel, thanks to Facebook, to buyers in Europe who happen to like that particular style. Demographics can help you find your target audience, or in some cases discover new customers in other parts of the world.

Using demographics such as these and those found at numerous other sites can help you zero in on your potential target market. You can also look for influencers on the various sites and check out their Klout or Kred scores to determine if they're influential to the audience with whom you want to engage.

Looking at the Numbers

So how popular is Facebook compared to the other social media platforms? As of December 2012, according to interviews conducted by Pew Research Center's Internet and Life Project, the percentage of Internet users on Facebook was more than the next four platforms combined. Facebook's 67 percent topped Twitter at 16 percent, Pinterest at 15 percent, Instagram at 13 percent, and Tumblr at 6 percent, or a combined total of 50 percent between the four next in line behind Facebook.

If you're thinking about your demographic audience, then it's important to take a closer look at who uses these popular platforms. Facebook, for example, is used by 72 percent women on the Internet, while 62 percent of men have Facebook pages. The highest percentage of users fall between the ages 18 and 29 at 85 percent, with 30- to 49-year-olds checking in at 73 percent. But for those of you who think Facebook is for the young at heart, consider that 57 percent of Internet users between ages 50 and 64 also use Facebook.

Twitter, meanwhile, has a slightly higher number of men than women on board with 17 percent of male internet users topping 15 percent of female users. There is also an interesting race/ethnic breakdown with black, non-Hispanics checking in at 26 percent, 19 percent for Hispanic users, and white, non-Hispanic users at 14 percent. Here, too, the largest percentage of users are the 18- to 29-year-olds at 27 percent, with a drop-off to 16 percent in the 30- to 49-year-old range.

And if you are visually minded and thinking of utilizing Pinterest to reach your target market, you'd best be thinking about reaching out to the ladies, since 25 percent of women on the Internet are on Pinterest compared to only 5 percent of men. You'll also find that there is a peak in the higher income levels for Pinterest, with 23 percent of the audience earning in the $50,000 to $74,999 range per household while other platforms mentioned are fairly consistent across income lines. Pinterest also has a higher percentage of their users coming from rural communities, while both Facebook and Twitter get more of their audience from the urban areas.

How to Build a Facebook Page for Your Small Business

Personal Facebook pages number in the millions and an increasing number of small business owners are establishing what Facebook calls "Fan Pages." You should start one for your small business because more than 5 million Facebook users a day become fans of various pages.

Here's how to do it:

1. Create your personal page first.
To create a "business" (or "fan") page, log into your personal account -- only logged in users can create a fan page -- then go to the following URL: www.facebook.com/pages/create.php.

2.   Determine what category your business falls into.
Brand? Product? Organization? Artist? Band? Public Figure? Pick the one that best fits your company.

3. Create your business page.
Post photos, contact information, services, products, etc.

4. Promote your business page.
Post a link to it from your personal page. Buy social ads on Facebook directing users to your business page. And promote your Facebook business page using Twitter, Linked In, and your email newsletter to customers, your website, and your blog.

5. Create a sub-domain of your Facebook business page (facebook.yourcompany.com) on your main domain that sends users to your Facebook business page.

6. Study Facebook ads and the specific demographics that will get buyers to your business page. For example, you can target various economic groups and geographical locations.

Twitter Tips for Your Business

With Twitter's restrictions for Tweets to adhere to a 140-character count limit, many businesses are employing their creative assets to set themselves apart from the crowd. But finding truly engaging content can be exhausting, especially when your main gig consists of running a business.

Here's how to add a little spice to your Tweets to enhance engagement:

1. Use photos.
Because a picture is worth a thousand words, sharing pictures on the micro-blogging network seems a viable solution. Twitter's latest design makes images more prominent, and that's something we can get behind. Make use of this new feature by sharing high quality images with your followers such as a behind-the-scenes look at your business, informative graphics for special offers, and much more.

2. Share videos.
We're in a video generation, and video is the newest approach to marketing strategy. Consider sharing videos that show a behind-the-scenes aspect of your business, giving your followers insights on what happens any given day. Also, keep your videos short and sweet as engagement often drops significantly after about 30 seconds. Vine and Instagram make it easy.

3. Include Quality Content.
If content is king, what's the queen? Many people say it's the research put forth in creating said content, while others say it's the context in which the content is delivered.

Whatever the "queen" of your content may be, there are a few factors that regulate what's quality and what's not. Content must be relevant, informative and valuable to those who are accessing it. Here are some tips to keep in mind when creating content for your small business:

- Quality content is jargon free. Your customers shouldn't have to decipher the meaning of your content.

- Quality content doesn't sound sales pitchy. Content shouldn't sound like an advertisement, but it does need to have a subtle marketing message that can be tied back to your business strategy.

- Quality content has an easy-to-read structure. You want your content to look appealing. Headers, sub-headings, bullet points, graphs, quotes, etc. help to organize your content.

- Quality content inspires action. Quality content addresses the needs of a specific audience. The content should pique the interest or stir emotion.

12 Ways to Increase Sales with Social Media

A conversion rate is the rate of viewers/visitors you can turn into actual customers. The higher your conversion rate, the more money you make. Here are 12 ways to increase your conversion rate...

1. Motivate with discounts, special offers and perks that are time sensitive, so visitors need to act quickly.

2. Post quality content that appeals to your target audience and a steady basis.

3. Test. Try various types of content, including images and videos.

4. Include customer comments, quotes and testimonials so that viewers will see that others like what you have to offer.

5. Keep postings short and to the point. Lengthy posts, cluttered pages, or too many hashtags limit engagement and, subsequently, conversions.

6. Offer an e-mail blog subscription or opt-in e-mail to keep your subscribers involved.
7. Remember the 80-20 rule that says 80 percent of your business will come from return customers. Sing the praises of your current customers, thank them, give them the inside lowdown, and make them feel wanted and appreciated. Happy customers lead to conversions.

8. Great headlines. No matter what the content is, use a headline that jumps out. If your conversion rate is not what you want it to be, change your headlines. Businesses have reported 100 percent increases in conversions by changing headlines!

9. Track your competitors. Any public-facing information is fair game and you can access such data to see what your competitors are doing to engage people. You can then strategize to do something better, or different, to improve your conversion rates.

10. Use calls to action that cite the benefit to potential buyers. For example, if you are trying to drum up orders for a money-making book, don't simply post "Order You Copy Now." Your call to action could also include, "More money means an increase to your quality of life."

11. Make your call to action larger or bolder than other content. Bright colors, for example, have seen better conversion rates.

12. Make every step of a conversion as easy as possible. Each step you add will lose conversions. Take a page from Amazon and keep it simple.

Advanced Social Media Tips and Tricks!

Do you want to be a Rookie or a Pro Bowl Veteran? The way you go about "tackling" your career is similar to being a rookie or a veteran. You can go through the day-to-day and remain average, or you can study, practice, train, and try to find every possible advantage you can over your opponents.

For me, these are simple things you must do to take part in everyday social media. To others, these might feel like advanced techniques and tactics that are at a higher knowledge level and maybe even desire level when it comes to doing social media. If you want to elevate your game to get the most out of your investment (time and money) in social media, then I highly recommend that you take it to the next level with these tips and tricks.

FACEBOOK
Trial Run: Test Engagement for Different Times of Day

A lot of companies post on Facebook only during traditional hours. But what if your constituents are mostly abroad? How about those night owls? Tap into your inner scientist and experiment by posting on your Facebook feed during different times throughout the day (and night). Different studies will point to different conclusions, but the truth is, results will vary depending on the kind of users your brand attracts. The only way to ensure optimal engagement is through old-fashioned trial and error. While I NEVER suggest anyone automate their posting, if you feel like you have to, Facebook now offers a scheduling tool so you can deliver late-night posts without disturbing your own beauty sleep. But keep in mind that when a company makes a post, people assume that there's someone there live. If you don't reply back or address the issue because it was a scheduled post and you aren't ACTUALLY there, you look bad.

Let the People Speak

Launching a new product? Deciding on a new design? Ask your fans their input and actually ACT on their feedback. Whether you ask them to vote on a new logo or product color, use their input to reasonably guide the direction of your next business decision. Not only will it increase your audience's brand loyalty, it also helps you get a sense of what your fan base wants.

Take a Picture -- It'll Last Longer

More importantly, pictures are shared more. In fact, one study showed that picture posts receive TWICE as much engagement as posts with just text or links. Fans' news feeds are constantly cluttered with friends and business pages, so including a photo or graphic with your content helps your post stand out. And you don't need an expensive camera: Download Instagram to your smartphone to instantly snap and upload shots to your Facebook page.

Be Your Own Biggest Fan

In order to fully understand the latest fads and trends on Facebook, you have to actually use Facebook outside of your business page. So if you haven't already, it's time to join the rest of the world and create a personal Facebook account. This will allow you to see how fans are seeing your own business as well as what the competition is doing, and how other users are innovating online.

Get Your Fans Off Facebook...

And onto your email list. By giving fans an incentive to subscribe to your email list, you can expand your touch points. Keep your Facebook content upbeat and FUN, while saving more targeted marketing and upselling for your email campaigns. The results will speak for themselves.

A Call to Action

Because you don't want your Facebook fans to visit once and then leave, place a "call-to-action" graphic on your page's tab. It can be something as simple as "Like Us!" with arrows pointing towards the like button. Make it easy for visitors to convert into fans by giving them every opportunity to add you to their feeds.

Hide and Seek

Make people want what you have: Create content that is exclusive to fans only, which will encourage visitors to like your page. This could be special product information, interviews, menus -- whatever fits in with your particular business.

There are a couple of ways to do it (and it keeps changing) via existing apps of custom FBML (Facebook Markup Language). Easiest method I've found is to do a Google search for "Static FBML app." Some of them have the built-in ability to provide exclusive content only to people who have liked your page.

Here's the coding:

```
<fb:fbml version="1.1">
<fb:visible-to-connection> information for fans only!
<fb:else> information for fans and non-fans!
```

But Be Easy to Find

Create a vanity URL for your Facebook business page. This makes you more discoverable, so your fans can just go to facebook.com/yourbusinessname. Just go to www.facebook.com/<your username> to update your business page name.

Post Weekly Pins

Not to be confused with a Pinterest pin, Facebook allows businesses to pick one post a week to be featured at the top of your page. So, whatever information you're trying to push each week, be it a sale or promotion or event, be sure to anchor it to the top of your timeline. It's very simple: Just hover over the post you've selected to anchor, click the pencil icon, and select "Pin to Top." These pins expire every seven days, which makes it a great way to highlight your most up-to-date posts.

Show Off Your Milestones

Facebook milestones don't just have to be about relationship updates or graduations. Highlight your company's accomplishments, whether it's an anniversary, meeting a fan growth goal, or launching a new product. You can create a milestone in the status update box, then fill in information such as date and location. And as always, be sure to add a picture with each one!

TWITTER
Follow the Leads

Twitter isn't just about your tweets; it's also a great source for information on your competition. But don't just follow your rivals; follow your rival's followers! This will give you fresh insight on how to broaden your own following and what those people are looking for. It may even show you what your competition is doing better than you. With a little tweet tweaking, you may be able to get those followers to convert to your own company.

Don't get caught up in using Twitter as a selling tool. Instead, use it to increase customer loyalty and offer valuable information for your followers. Over marketing will merely leave a sour taste in followers' mouths, and you may even end up losing them if their feed gets too clogged with too many promotions.

Keep It Short

Posting links and content is a great thing, but Twitter users are all about brevity, so be sure to shorten your links by using a redirect service. http://bit.ly and http://is.gd are good ones to use, but there are other companies that offer additional services. Take a few minutes to do some research and find the best fit for your brand.

Reply with a Period

Twitter filters allow users to only view replies if they are following each side of the conversation. But by starting off your reply with a period, that post won't start with @, it will instead be viewed as a separate tweet and will be seen by all of your followers. Breaking grammar rules never felt so good.

Lose a Few Characters

Yes, 140 characters is the technical limit on Twitter, but all the cool kids are now only tweeting with 125 or less. Short, punchy tweets will grab your followers' attention rather than getting lost in their feeds.

Twitter + & =???

Lose the ampersand in both your profile and your tweets: Whatever the reason, Twitter doesn't display the "&" sign correctly, so save your followers the trouble of trying to figure out what it says and just spell out the word; it's worth the extra two characters.

Cross-Post to Facebook

Kill two birds with one stone by connecting your Twitter feed to your Facebook account. Head to your Twitter profile settings, then go to the bottom of the page underneath your bio. It's an easy way to have your tweets post automatically to your Facebook feed.

A Picture's Worth a Thousand Tweets

I can't stress enough how important pictures are in and social media platform, and Twitter is no exception. Use Twitpic to share photos as part of your tweets. Snapping photos on the go? Download the Twitterrific app to your smartphone to post pictures when you're away from the computer.

Nobody Likes a Qwitter

Qwitter is a great tool that notifies you when someone unfollows you on Twitter, and even goes as far as to suggest potential tweets that caused them to leave. There are both free and "pro" memberships available, depending on how often you want information and how detailed you'd like it.

YOUTUBE
Maximize Video Descriptions

Don't just use your YouTube video description to talk about the video content; be sure to share links to your website, Facebook page, Twitter account, and Pinterest page. And think carefully about keywords that will optimize search results leading to your video.

Keep It Private -- at First

It may sound crazy to initially publish your video as private, but videos take a while to process even after uploading. That means viewers can see these low-quality videos, rather than the actual final product! Give your video time to process before you make it public; you won't regret it.

Annotate Each Video

YouTube's annotation feature helps you interact with viewers as they are watching your video. Add comments or links that will come up at predetermined intervals. All of the timing and content is decided by you, making this a completely customizable function.

Extend Your Reach by Podcasting

Another way to cross-market your YouTube videos is to upload them on iTunes as podcasts. Millions of viewers tune in to podcasts daily, making this a great way to target new audience members. There are plenty of free podcasting hosts and publishers, making it cheap and easy to give your videos extra exposure.

File Name Optimization

While you may be inclined to put the most amount of thought into your video title, YouTube actually weighs file names more heavily than titles. Giving your file name, an optimized title is a quick, easy way to tag your videos in user searches.

Video Transcription

Here's another SEO tip to increase your video rankings. Add a transcription of your video's audio. It's actually quite easy once you've created the plain text document. Simply click the "captions" button, then click "Upload caption file to transcript."

Customize Your Channel Background

This is an easy trick if you've got even the most basic graphic design skills (or a few extra bucks to hire someone). By creating a customized background or frame for your YouTube page, you encourage viewers to stay on your channel and browse for other videos. Click on your username, then "My Channel." Then select "Themes and Colors" where you can upload your image.

Give Yourself Credit

Sharing is a big part of succeeding on YouTube, or any social media platform, for that matter. But what happens when someone tries to take your video and pass it off as their own? While your video may continue to be shared, no one will relate it to you or your brand. So take a quick extra step by stamping your website URL as a watermark on your video. This makes it much more difficult for people to claim it as their own original content, and even if it is shared beyond your YouTube channel, your business gets some automatic marketing. This feature should be available in just about any video editing software you use.

Integrate and Embed

Videos take a long time to make, so don't silo yours on YouTube alone. Embed videos on your Facebook page and provide a link on Twitter. Your followers may only be active on one or two platforms, but that doesn't mean they don't want all the information you have to offer. Always make it as easy as possible to provide your fans with your valuable content.

Brand Your Channel

Just like any other marketing channel you use; your YouTube channel and videos should reflect your brand's tone. Be consistent with how you portray yourself so that viewers recognize who you are among the competition. It is particularly important to create a sense of cohesion among all of your social media platforms. Be integrated in every sense of the word.

PINTEREST
Tag, You're It

It's not enough to simply pin your own images and hope others will repin. You must also actively engage with others by repinning content. A good way to gain new followers is to tag the original pinner in the description section. All you have to do is add the @ symbol in front of their name, and they will know that you mentioned them. Let's face it, it's flattering to know that our pins are being used by others and adding the small touch of specifically referencing the pinner is a great way to gain a loyal following on Pinterest.

Put a Price on It

Pinterest users are not just on the site to find inspiration -- they're also there to shop. If you're selling a product, or even repinning products that are relevant to your business, be sure to include a price tag on the image because these pins get 36 percent more likes than those without price tags. So even if you're not selling your own products, think of creative ways to incorporate products with keywords that pinners will search for. If you're a designer, create a mood board; if you offer styling services, pin seasonal looks from online retailers. Think outside the box to maximize likes and repins through product pinning.

Search Simply

Pinterest search analytics are far less complicated than those of Google and other web search engines. When uploading original content, be sure to use strong keywords as part of the image's file name. So rather than keeping the camera's generic "1MG 4289," customize it to reflect what you are trying to sell, like "round brilliant cut engagement ring.jpg." Even if you're promoting a concept rather than a product, you can still use this SEO technique to your benefit.

Get Verified

Show pinners that you are a trustworthy source by verifying your business. It's a very simple process on Pinterest's website that simply confirms your website. Not only can users see that you are verified, it also gives you access to Pinterest's analytics, which can give you a lot of insight on what you're doing right and ways you may need to improve.

Speaking of Analytics...

Check out Pinterest's "Web Analytics Walkthrough" video, which shows you how to measure your metrics and conversions. You'll be able to tell how many pinners visited your website for your Pinterest page, how popular your pins are, and what is being repinned from your website. Knowledge is power; make sure you have the most information possible about what's going on in your Pinterest page and external website.

Focus Groups

Checking out pinners who follow your business can give you a lot of valuable information about your target consumers. By following these pinners and evaluating what else they are pinning, liking, and commenting on, you can glean detailed trends about your audience.

Visually Market Your Content

Even if you're not selling a physical product, Pinterest can help market your brand. Pin industry info graphics, charts, slides, or other visual elements. Also, be sure to use photos on your blog or website so that people visiting can pin those images as well.

Provide Useful Information

This is another great tip for content-oriented businesses: Pin ideas or products that would be useful to your target audience. Have you read a good business book recently? Pin it! Do you know of a helpful YouTube video on public speaking? Pin it! Be a resource to your constituents by providing useful, relevant information and ideas.

Guess What This Next Tip Is?

Start a conversation in the comments section by adding a question to your pin's description. It could be as simple as, "Guess what this is?" or an open-ended question about your business like, "Tell us what you think about..." By giving pinners an opportunity to comment, you're far more likely to create an engaging environment. And while I'm on the subject, remember your manners and comment back. The goal here is to be a hub of interaction for pinners and potential clients.

Board Focus

Create boards on whatever topics are relevant to your business or brand and start pinning images. Lowe's, for example, has boards such as "Helpful Hints," "Patio Paradise," and "Curb Appeal." Seasonal boards are also a good idea and be sure to more actively populate the current time of year.

For Analytics Junkies

If Pinterest's business analytics just aren't enough for you, there are a number of programs for businesses that allow you to track pins in real-time, analyze your followers, or even help you upload and schedule your pins in advance. Here are a few outline resources for those who really want to catapult their "pinfluence":

www.Piqora.com

www.PinAlerts.com

www.Pinreach.com

www.HelloInsights.com

www.Pingraphy.com

Successful Promotional Letters & Marketing!

A promotional letter is one that introduces plugs or promotes a product or service. Normally it offers something "not available in stores" and invites this response: "we will send you a wonderful 'X' if you will send us your check, your Visa number, or your authorization to bill you later for an amazing, low bargain price." Normally the offer throws in a few extras, "absolutely free."

If done well, most readers who do not throw the offer into the trash without reading it should be greatly tempted. Perhaps driven by greed, unrequited sex drive, or the saintly quest for universal truth, the reader will send the requested money. He will get his product, and hopefully he will be pleased; at least enough so that he will purchase from you again, or not return the product.

Any promotional mailing, once it reaches the prospect's mailbox, is called "Junk Mail" by the uninformed masses. In truth, writing successful marketing letters is nothing less than an art form. A beautifully composed letter will get a strong gut response just like a masterpiece of art or music. Fortunately, you can be a master marketer with a lot less talent than it takes to become Beethoven or Picasso. Savvy marketing is perhaps the most powerful and potentially high-earning skill anyone can have.

The same talent for writing an effective mail order offer can be used for writing effective radio, TV or classified advertising offers. They are all a part of the same bag, though different tricks of the trade must be employed for different media.

Not Available In Stores...

When a product is "not available in stores," people are tempted. It may be something good. But they also need to be especially motivated to send away their hard-earned cash to an unknown vendor. Although the reputation of mail order marketers is not nearly as bad as it was years ago, most people prefer "cash and carry." They would rather see and touch something before they buy it.

"I'm not a crook."

Richard Nixon, disgraced president of our country, gave us these immortal words. You want to convince your customers you are not a crook, but just saying it doesn't do the trick. There are other, more subtle ways of establishing your credibility.

When an individual or small, unknown company is making a direct mail offer, the reader is naturally wary. His money may disappear without any response. The buyer might not get anything nearly as good as the described products he visualized. A mail order sale always carries the risk that the money will be banked by some fly-by-night who doesn't bother to send out any goods. This is fraud. If a swindler gets caught, he can do time for mail fraud. Actually, there are fewer mail frauds of this type than in past years. Why? Because financial frauds and other criminal activities are easier to pull off.

Here I'm teaching you how to make serious money in an honest, legal way. Part of making money in an honest way involves convincing your customers you are honest. This a part of your pitch in a promotional letter. Here are a few more suggestions to relax the fear that your particular offer might be a petty fraud. If and when you become a writer of promotional letters, you'll have to be extremely creative to, among other things, create trust in the reader's mind. You'll also have to avoid obvious manifestations of the fly-by-night syndrome.

1. Avoid the use of a PO Box. This should be an obvious thing to remember. The reality is that it is exceedingly easy to get a mail drop with a street, address, but the public doesn't know this. The average person will feel a street address is real and permanent while a box number is the opposite.

2. Accept credit cards or online orders/payments via PayPal.

3. Your message on the letter itself should contain a personal element or story to get empathy and suspend natural skepticism.

Learn how to write an effective direct mail appeal.

Promotional letters probably fill your mailbox just about every day. You don't need me to tell you what they look like. You can read them carefully and judge for yourself the difference between a good pitch and a letter that is failure. Within a few days you should be able to write a good promotional letter. If you feel that getting more marketing skills is important to you, go online for more info and/or start reading books by the masters, like Joe Cossman and Jay Abraham.

Insider Insights

When planning any marketing campaign, it is a good idea to make a guesstimate of your costs and profits. This is part of the "sound business plan" that lenders and investors are always so impressed with. Still, if your product or slant is new and original, you won't know how it will work until you test it with a small classified ad or small mailing. Yet there are certain rules of thumb. From the point of view of the sender, with an average price product that an average person can afford, a two percent return rate on promotional letters to a "good" mailing list is average. A five percent rate is phenomenal.

Will you make a fortune offering something that is very expensive in mail order? Probably not. But Jay Abraham, a mail order marketing genius, regularly offers seminars priced from $2,000 to $10,000 on mail order by mail order. His target lists are those mail order marketers who are already successful, but who want to do better. High ticket items are normally sold through direct contact made after a promotional letter has elicited some interest. Abraham or a member of his staff talks to the most potential customers on the phone to close the sell.

Usually promo letters (without any telephone follow up) are used for selling things in the $10 to $100 range. Newsletter and magazine subscriptions, inspirational books and music CDs are all common mail order promo ad items. The vast majority of the so-called junk mail letters in your daily post are genuine. Send the money and you will have received the advertised product. Most companies will promptly honor stated refund policies. They don't want complaints to the postal authorities. Also, they hope to keep you on their mailing list and sell you other products. A customer who has received good service is usually a satisfied customer and will look at other forms from the same source.

Finding A Suitable Product To Market

How can you make money from promotional letters? Assuming you want to do it the honest way, you must find or create a product. That is not as difficult as you think. You may already have one. If so, here is what is important to remember:

GET MONEY: Self-Educate, Get Rich & Enjoy Life, Vol. 1

To make any money, an item sold by mail order must have a four-to-one markup to break even after advertising, promotional letter cost, packing, mailing and postage. That is the general rule of thumb.

How Ordinary People Learned To Write Effective Promo Letters

You must learn to write an effective letter, and have it mechanically reproduced. But how is this talent learned? You can always copy others' ideas, but in the end, you must carve out a special place, a style of your own. The best advice is to learn by doing and to get your education in the school of hard knocks as just about every successful hustler or tycoon has done. The most important thing to remember is that the best copywriters are not academic types. They use bad grammar like, "Doublemint Gum Tastes Good like a Good Gum Should." If you didn't recognize that a proper sentence would have ended with the word "taste," you are on the right track and have a good chance of writing successful advertising copy!

One lady, Harriet Walters, was an ambitious 19-year-old without any resources when she graduated from College. She approached various charities with a proposal to write a promo letter about their good works. The letter would make a pitch for tax deductible donations. Harriet would get the standard fund-raiser deal; a third of all funds raised. As it turned out, Harriet became a very successful fund raiser for charity.

Her idea was original and simple. She'd enclose with the pitch a "free gift" to make the recipient feel guilty about ripping off a wonderful charitable organization. So, for an orphanage for poor African kids she sent off a small plastic replica of an African doll. Of course, the letter still had to be a real heart-wrenching tear jerker. For diseases, she sent off air mail and other stickers saying in tiny print, "I saved a child from leukemia."

She's been at the game for decades now and her gross annual collections are in the fifty-million-dollar range. Two-thirds goes to the charity, one-third to her. The charities are happy with the arrangement as they go from nickel-and-dime outfits, when she takes them on as a client, to the big time. There is no rule that says that people who work for charities and non-profit organizations can't be paid well. The head of the Red Cross is one of the highest paid executives in the world, and the Pope doesn't live like a bum either.

If you need a final example, executives of the United Nations from African countries, where the annual wage is under $100, average over $500,000 a year, plus expenses, plus whatever they can steal once they wangle a job in New York or Geneva. If you want to get seriously rich, get into government, religion or charity work! Harriet still does this work, only now with the aid of a huge staff of hired hands.

Can you hit the big time? One Russian tried raising funds for a little religious (Hebrew) school he ran in his living room for six neighborhood kids. He prepared a promotional letter sending out appeals for financial support by placing the letters under the doors of other recent immigrants.

They didn't work very well. So, he began writing "public service announcements" for New York TV and radio stations making a pitch for donations. These brought in such a good response that he decided to reinvest the funds raised to purchase advertising spots. His announcements about his school and its activities were written to sound like public service appeals. This format gave them a certain institutional quality and the implied endorsement of the TV station.

But why purchase air time if it's already something you can get for free? Here's why. Public service announcements come on in the AM or at such similar times when the listening audience is at its lowest ebb. There are no paying customers for these spots, so the stations give them away. The Rabbi knew you always get what you pay for and what you get as a gift is usually worth what you paid. Our hero, who by this time is calling himself a Rabbi, but really isn't, even grows curls and looks the part.

With another idea, he became as rich as a sweepstakes lottery winner. How? By registering his non-profit Hebrew school for young children as a charity, and then coming up with a unique and original fund-raising pitch. "Donate your used car to Rabbi Lubin's School and get a tax deduction for more than the value of the car. You will get a receipt from a registered charity that gives you more cash in your hand (after tax savings) than if you sold the car!"

What happened to the cars? The Rabbi kept a few for himself and his friends but sold the rest.

At a stroke, he became the third largest car dealer in the US. The cars are sold at bargain prices, usually a quarter of their "appraised tax value." The Rabbi who just got off the boat from Russia couldn't read or write English. His school is as small as ever, but he is affluent, all despite criticism from newspapers (including the Wall Street Journal) that he is abusing his charitable status for personal gain. To this criticism, he answers in a jolly, good-natured way, "Vell, ven a new mensch makes good, zer are always gonna be doze people who are jealous."

Get the idea? Get money!

 # How to Maximize Marketing Dollars!

1. Introduction: How to Maximize your Budget

It's the kind of challenge that can keep you up at night. As a small business owner, you need marketing to generate increased sales and income. But when sales and income are constrained, your marketing capacity is limited -- just when you need that capacity most. The solution isn't as elusive as it seems: there are ways to market effectively on a budget, experts say. In fact, you can do it productively even when your company's budget doesn't include a line item for marketing.

Every piece of communication that you send out is a marketing opportunity. Make documents exciting that otherwise might be boring. Make them fun; put them to work. That includes your email signature line, which you can use to promote upcoming events, new products or services, or your social media pages.

2. Redefine Marketing and Reinvigorate Sales

Another productive strategy that costs you nothing more than a change in perspective. See, most people think about their marketing as getting new leads. Yet in marketing, the most expensive place to sell is to a new customer. To recapture business from old customers, contact them during down times and offer "a specific reason" for them to purchase from you again. And when you do pursue new leads, enlist the help of your best customers by soliciting referrals instead of relying passively on word of mouth.

Don't forget to solicit social media reviews. Endorsements from "real people" now carry more weight than traditional marketing messages. Whether you run a dry cleaner, an accounting firm, or a general contracting company, a customer who refers to you as "my" service provider is your best promoter, they say.

Some small business owners worry that soliciting reviews puts unwanted pressure on customers and can contain good relationships, but you don't have to word it in a way that says, 'Leave me a good review'. Just email those customers that you have a good relationship with and ask for a review. That does amazing things for your SEO, as well, once you start racking up those good reviews.

3. Track Results for Repeat Success

What's the best marketing strategy for the budget you do have? The challenge I find with most small business owners is they have no real, reliable way that they track their marketing. To create your marketing roadmap, you need to know how to calculate your return on past marketing investments.

Let's say that last year, you invested $1,000 in a pay-per-click campaign that generated 100 leads. You also spent $10,000 to exhibit at a trade show that generated 1,000 leads. That means that with each marketing strategy, you spent $10 per lead. Now, that doesn't tell you how good the lead is, so you need the second number, which is your cost per sale. That will tell you how good the lead quality is. Your second step, then, is to look at how many of your leads from each marketing campaign resulted in a sale.

Once you have that number, you can compare the value of the sale with the cost of the campaign. You can set up a simple spreadsheet to do all this, so the math is already pre-done. This is called your ROI per $1 invested.

This formula attaches a hard number to the value of a given marketing strategy and compares that number with the results produced by other strategies. Tracking those results helps you to project the most profitable use of your marketing budget going forward.

Your company's challenge will be greater if you're in startup mode or haven't tracked your past marketing performance. What's more, your mileage may vary from one year or even one quarter to another. But whatever your starting point, it's essential to collect and analyze each of these factors to develop a more predictable and profitable marketing strategy.

4. Build your Budget and your Sales

Once you've decided what you can spend, how do you convert that raw number into a budget that will work as hard as it can for your business? Here is a six-step plan...

Step 1. Review your data, identify those with the highest ROI, and then determine which can be expanded. For example, if you've had huge success at a trade show, but it's the only one in your industry, then additional trade shows aren't an option.

Step 2. Once you've selected targets for expansion, record a results projection.

Step 3. Create a plan for tracking results going forward, and establish a schedule for reviewing those numbers to check them against your projections.

Step 4. Develop a marketing calendar, which is probably the best internal control you have that ensures you don't screw up the dates. Start with hard dates, such as the trade show schedule or the date that a direct mailer must go out, and work backward from there to determine your internal deadlines.

Step 5. Pull the trigger and implement it.

Step 6. Review, at least once a quarter, how it went. Look at your scorecard to make adjustments going forward to optimize the use of your cash. And that's how you maximize your marketing dollars.

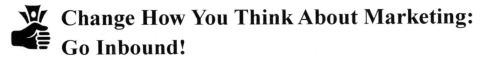 Change How You Think About Marketing: Go Inbound!

Creating and sharing useful content can help you attract and retain customers. Some entrepreneurs think marketing is a necessary evil. You may be one of them. But when it's right, it's the engine that will help your business grow.

Yes, I know you're going to build a killer product that people are going to love. Marketing can help you find people to love it. And, yes, you can hire a PR agency and hope for "free" publicity. That's fine -- but what are you going to do during the other 363 days? You need to invest in marketing.

The trick is honing in on the right kind of marketing. The best marketing is inbound, which is basically doing what you do best: helping customers. Inbound marketing is about creating content that is useful for your potential customers and using it as a tool to bring people in.

Startups and small businesses should not participate in an arms race for attention. You won't win by shouting louder, getting bigger ads or buying a bigger booth at the trade show. In fact, you can't: Your larger competitors have massive marketing budgets, and you will never be able to outspend them. As a small business, you need to find marketing that gives you leverage with your disproportionate, long-term returns given the investment.

Inbound marketing focuses on attracting people by providing value instead of pushing your way in. The most common way to do this is to create content that is helpful, optimize that content and spread it.

Great content can come in a number of forms. The most common and useful include blogs, photos, info graphs, videos, podcasts, presentations, e-books, software and tools. When creating content think about the type of information that will be most helpful for your customers. Relevant and useful content makes people happy.

The next step is to optimize that content for search engines. Did you know that there are nearly 6 billion searches on Google every day? Maybe a few of those people would be interested in your product. Basic search engine optimization can help maximize the potential of those searches and drive organic traffic to your site.

After you've created content and optimized it, you have to spread it. Social media can help. It takes some time, but it's a great way to make that awesome content you're producing and spread it farther. Keep in mind that the easier your content is to share; the more people will share it.

By creating content specifically designed to appeal to your dream customers, inbound marketing attracts qualified prospects to your business and keeps them coming back for more.

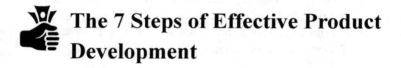 The 7 Steps of Effective Product Development

Developing a successful product line doesn't have to be a fumble in the dark. Here are seven best practices for bringing your baby to market as efficiently and economically as possible...

1. Solicit Feedback. Now.

It's not enough to run nascent products by family and friends. Instead, vet early-stage plans and photo types with potential customers (in other words, strangers). The idea is to get people to tell you whether the product meets their needs and, if not, what might improve it. Is the product the right shape? Are buttons or other functional components in the right place? Is it the right color? Does it perform the way people want it to? Figure this out now so that you're not spending weeks or months working on features that might not even matter to your customers.

2. Refine Your Design with Simplicity in Mind.

A straightforward product design is essential. The same goes for brand continuity among every item you sell.

Your product has to capture someone's attention within the first three seconds of glancing at it. In fact, quality design is the best investment you can make.

Product packaging should be clean and compelling as well, with easy-to-read text. Busy packaging that explodes with colors or design elements will only frustrate customers.

In most consumer product categories, packaging is your only communication with customers. People need to know what you're selling from 30 feet away.

When developing packaging, consider where your products will be sold. Retailers want packaging that won't take up too much space, and many are looking for eco-friendly options. Get this right, because the cost of redoing it is not cheap.

3. Don't Skimp on Materials or Manufacturing.

A low-cost vendor isn't necessarily your best bet. It's important not to make purchasing decisions based solely on price. You have to go for quality and reputation. That may mean spending a little extra, given that top-shelf suppliers, labs and manufacturers tend to charge more.

Look online, attend trade shows and collect industry recommendations. You may need to hire an agent to find a factory for you; however, you must personally visit any factory you're thinking of partnering with, even if it's 8,000 miles away.

To ensure that product is up to snuff, create guidelines for every manufacturing detail. It's not enough to outline 85 percent of the process. For example, don't simply say that your product should be constructed of stainless steel – ¬specify 'A' grade, or the factory will likely use the lowest-end option.

Don't expect a flawless product off the bat and stay on top of every detail. You have to check that. It's like a Grand Canyon-size cliff if you don't. Because that's your opportunity to sign off that your product is correct, and if it's not, to have the production line stop and fix it.

4. Price it Right.

Many entrepreneurs fail to factor in all overhead costs -- including shipping and duties -- when considering pricing. Other mistakes: gauging incorrectly what consumers will be willing to pay, not knowing where you want to sell the product and thinking you can make the same profit margin from high- and low-end retailers. For example, selling at Nordstrom will yield a different margin than selling on Amazon and may require different packaging.

Wait to do the math until you've nailed down all the particulars. Once you run the numbers, if your profit margins are too low (or the price you need to charge to make a profit is too high), you may need to whittle down your manufacturing costs.

Look to the marketplace -- at comparable products and industry margins -- to calculate product price. I've always been a big believer that your costs are driven by the market, unless you are creating a new market for a product.

If you need help setting prices, enlist the services of a product development consultant or sales broker.

5. Don't Overstock.

Sure, you don't want to run out of product. And sure, suppliers offer discounts for larger orders. But tying up all your capital in inventory can turn your company into the Titanic. If you think you're going to sell 100 pieces, don't go buy 1,000. Instead, buy 110.

Cash flow, shipping time, storage space and shelf life will dictate how much product you stock. It's an intricate dance, and every industry is different.

Then there's the matter of how many colors, styles, sizes and other variations you offer. Again, fewer are better. Give consumers too many options, and you risk overwhelming them. There's that old adage: A confused mind won't buy.

6. Protect your Ideas.

Intellectual property laws can protect you only if you arm yourself accordingly. Hiring a tough IP attorney is a must. But before you shell out thousands, visit the U.S. Patent and Trademark Office website (uspto.gov) to learn about these protections and ensure your idea hasn't already been patented or trademarked by someone else.

As early as possible, you should trademark your product name, purchase the corresponding web domain and file a provisional patent application, which won't break the bank but will allow you to stake a claim on your idea while giving you a year to file a formal application.

You probably won't be able to afford to patent your products in multiple countries from day one -- you'll likely file a U.S. patent first and add others as it makes sense. But it helps to determine early on where else you may want to market your idea, because once you head down this path, the deadlines for filing patents abroad arrive very quickly.

7. Consider Retailers and Communicate Wisely.

Landing a meeting with a potential retailer? You need to anticipate all questions they might lob your way, so you can help them see how to market and sell your product to their particular customer base. It's all about specify.

Keep your pitch simple. The most effective pitches usually relay three concise, memorable selling points for potential buyers. Put yourself in their shoes and know that they report to someone. You don't want your presentation to be overly complex.

You may not get into your preferred retail outlet your first time out. If that's the case, be persistent but pleasant. Follow up once a month or quarter with buyers you've met who are still on the fence.

Be wary of diving into the big-box pool too soon -- you need high profit margins to do so. Many retail chains will demand that you carry a hefty liability insurance policy and provide display boxes or fixtures for your products. You have to spend money to make money. And you have to make sure you have enough to spend

How One Company Turned Their Mission Statement into Big Bucks!

"This is your life. Do what you love and do it often. If you don't like something, change it. If you don't like your job, quit. If you don't have enough time, stop watching TV. If you are looking for the love of your life, stop; they will be waiting for you when you start doing things you love. Stop over-analyzing, life is simple. All emotions are beautiful. When you eat, appreciate every last bite. Open your mind, arms, and heart to new things and people, we are united in our differences. Ask the next person you see what their passion is and share your inspiring dream with them. Travel often; getting lost will help you find yourself. Some opportunities only come once, seize them. Life is about the people you meet, and the things you create with them, so go out and start creating. Life is short. Live your dream and share your passion."

Most mission statements contain words like value and service but often fail to explain what the founders truly care about, much less inspire anyone else to care. Holstee's mission statement is an exception. The Brooklyn, New York-based Company which sells eco-friendly clothing and accessories, rose from obscurity last year after its statement, dubbed the Holstee manifesto, and went viral. The document has been viewed online more than 50 million times and translated into 12 languages.

When Holstee turned the message into a $25 poster -- printed on recycled paper, of course -- the item quickly became one of the company's top sellers. Holstee's co-founders, Fabian Pfortmuller and Brothers Mike and Dave Radparvar, were as surprised as anyone that their mission statement, once tucked away on the About Us page of Holstee's website, resonated so strongly with so many people. Here is a quick interview with Pfortmuller about the impact a strong mission statement can have on a company.

How did you come up with your mission statement?

We wrote it a few months after we started Holstee, in 2009. We were talking about how every entrepreneur, including us, wants to build a lifestyle for himself. But even though you're your own boss, sometimes a start-up becomes something you can't control. You build your business, but at the end of the day, you might not even want to work there. So, we wanted to define what success means to us in nonmonetary terms.

We also knew that down the road, it would help to have a reminder of why we started Holstee.

Dave and Mike quit their jobs in the middle of a recession to start the company. The manifesto was a reminder that we took all these risks for a reason, to live a lifestyle we loved.

How did it get so big?

Two bloggers picked it up. That just kicked off a chain reaction. We saw it all over Tumblr and Twitter. People started making it their Facebook photo. We were so surprised at how people responded to it. I think society is just hungry for genuine values.

Whose idea was it to turn the manifesto into merchandise?

Actually, customers started asking for it. At first, we were hesitant about putting it on a poster. It was really personal to us and putting anything on a big poster or T-shirt can cheapen it. But we got so many requests that one of our freelancers convinced us to try it. We got amazing feedback. We sold about 11,000 posters last year [$25 x 11,000 = $275,000!]. They accounted for roughly 50 percent of our revenue in November.

How has the popularity of the posters influenced your brand?

Usually people make a product first, then build a brand around it. In our case, it happened the other way around. That has helped us build trust with our customers. People see the manifesto and automatically understand what we stand for. Then again, we're not a manifesto company, whatever that would be. The success of the posters helped us bootstrap, but at the end of the day, we're about products with a unique story that are designed with a conscience.

There are a lot of great lines in there. What's your favorite?

"Life is about the people you meet and the things you create with them." I strongly believe

that. Here at Holstee, I have the luck of working with my two best friends. We live together. We work together. We really live that.

Do you have any advice for business owners who want to create an inspiring mission statement?

Write it for yourself. Mission statements of large organizations sound meaningless, because

they're written to convince an audience. It's going to work only if it's genuine. We had selfish reasons for creating Holstee. We wanted to create great products, but we also wanted to have fun doing it. For us, it was more genuine to write about a lifestyle. If we can do all those things we mentioned, like travel, eat well, and build strong relationships, we'll be happier and build a better company because of it.

Note from Mike: This story inspired me and gave me a new perspective about ways to build a lifestyle brand. In my opinion, their story/experience is the essence of that. Via T-shirts and greeting cards, they're making a very nice income off their mission statement alone. Brilliant.

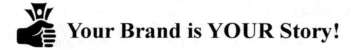
Your Brand is YOUR Story!

Branding is one of the major pain points for entrepreneurs. On the outside it seems simple, but its core is complex.

How can I become a great brand? How can I make this brand sustainable? What will bring value to my brand? Just what is my story, and how do I tell it? And, my favorite question and the most important by far: What the hell is branding?

Branding is more than a logo. It's more than a website. It's more than a business card. It's more than the colors and typefaces you chose to represent your company. Your brand is your voice in the marketplace, and it is your proposition for disruption. It is your opportunity to create something with lasting impact. It is how you tell your story, and it is absolutely key to your success and your survival.

Most entrepreneurs go to market not with a brand, buy with an idea -- an idea that can be so soulful and personal that it can be challenging to present and explain to others. You think everyone should intrinsically understand it, as you do -- but they don't. And that's why you need to develop effective brand messaging.

One of the most frequent comments I hear is, "People just don't understand us, our value and what we do, but we are absolutely the best at it." That statement is a problem. Your brand is your story, and if you can't tell it, then nobody will get it.

If you ever catch yourself making that sort of statement, tale a step back. Because it is total BS. No one is that special. This is business, not Dr. Phil, and if you cannot communicate the value of what you bring to the market, the economy and the world, well then, you have a problem.

Branding is about knowing what you stand for and how you communicate the values and character of your product or service. As a company founder, this is not so much a design choice as it is a leadership decision. Your job as chief is to know exactly, concisely and in context what you stand for. You are the lone author of your story, your mission and your reason for being. How you tell it is your job.

The Cell Block Presents TCB University

Part Two: Mailbox Money

How to Get the Most from Your Reports!

No other business venture seems so inviting or attracts so many people than that of selling via mail order. On the surface, it appears to be an easier and faster way to become rich than almost any other method of doing business. All the people in the world are your potential customers; you work from the privacy and comfort of your own home; you set your own working hours; and you answer to no one but yourself.

Ideally, you should have a product of your own, something you can produce at very low cost, and sell at top price. If you are buying something, advertising and reselling it, in order to realize a profit, you have to mark it up at least 500%. This is not an unreasonable markup for mail order sales.

Your product has to have mass appeal, and it has to be something not readily available to your prospective customers except through you. The product should be such that you can carry an inventory without worry of spoilage, aging or other damage. It should be something you can send through the mail, deliver to your customer, for next to nothing in relation to your selling price.

The best moneymaking product of all is a "How-to" report such as this one. You don't have to be a literary genius, or even an experienced writer to write one of these reports. In fact, the easiest way is to buy a set of these reports, read each one over, set it aside and write a similar one with more elaboration or from a different point of view. Give your report a commercially appealing title, set a price for it, advertise it widely in a number of nationally circulated mail order publications, and you could have something that will continue to bring in money for you for many years to come.

The absolute best money-maker of them all is a report you have found a great need for, researched thoroughly, and written from scratch. Discovering these needs is not that difficult a task.

If you just don't have the time to write and market one of these reports, or just cannot produce one for whatever reason, the next best thing is to purchase a set of these reports with reproduction rights. Here, you can have a number reprinted for as little as one to two cents each, and sell them for one to five dollars each. The only problem with this approach is that after a year, nearly everyone in mail order will have a copy of these reports and will be trying just as hard as you are to sell them.

Now, if you have bought the reproduction rights to the reports, you simply rewrite them put new titles on them, make up a new advertising circular, and send them out as new reports each year. There are a number of mail order self-help reports that have been making the rounds for the past 25 years in just this manner.

Just because you haven't got the time or the tools to write one of these reports is no reason for not producing one. If you have an idea or the background material, and the confidence that such a report will sell, get in touch with someone who specializes in this kind of writing, and have them put the finished product together for you. Generally, the fees will run to $100 per page. But this is an "incidental fee" indeed, if you come up with something that has the potential of bringing in several thousand dollars per year for the next ten years or so.

Remember, once you have it together and written, you just continue making copies of your original and filling prepaid cash orders for as long as you wish to stay in business.

You should also have advertising circulars, a catalog or a "follow-up" offer for every order you get. Many people make the mistake of "sending their whole store" in response to every inquiry. When you receive an inquiry to your advertising, you should have a prepared sales letter describing the item you're advertising, and perhaps a circular which lists in catalog style some of your other products that tie in with the product of your sales letter. This is known as the "Featured Selection plus Alternates" approach.

When you receive an order for the product you've been advertising or featuring in your mail efforts, include one of your product catalogs in the package with the customer's order. The most effective practice is to include an advertising circular or brochure of a leader item or special-of-the-month, and your catalog. The main thing NOT to do is to include more than a couple of separate "featured selection" circulars. Keep your eyes on how the big mail order houses do it and duplicate their operating plan within your own means.

The important point to remember here is to be sure to include something different, something new, something your customer has not seen or been offered a chance to buy, with each successive contact you make with him. Once you've broken the ice and got him spending money with you, continue showing him products of a related nature that should stimulate his appetite for more. For sure, he will never be more in the mood to buy from you than when he receives something he has ordered. So, every time you fill and send out an order to a buyer, include an opportunity for him to buy even more from you.

You can make a very comfortable income, but you will never get rich so long as you're having your orders drop shipped for you. Having a connection with a prime source that will drop ship orders for you is one of the surest and best ways to "learn" the business of selling by mail, but if you really want to make it big, you will use drop shipping sources for learning, and for backing up your primary product with follow-up offers. If you don't have a primary product of your own, the next best thing is to buy in quantity lots at wholesale prices. A word of caution here, however: Do not buy a quantity supply of anything until you have seen a sample of the product and have thoroughly tested the salability of that product. Too often, the beginner is sold a quantity of a certain product at so-called wholesale prices, only to find that after he has spent his capital he either doesn't want to put forth the effort and time to sell that particular product, or that he can't "give it away", let alone sell it. Suppliers who operate this way, almost forcing you to buy an inventory to have available for your order, generally derive most of their income from the sale of the initial "required" inventories.

Always investigate and check out the salability before you buy anything more than just a single sample.

Selling your reports depends on your advertising. You have to get the word out that you have "money-making information" available for sale. Start out small by using short classified ads. Look at how some of the established mail-order-report sellers are doing it and copy their methods. Do not copy their ads; instead, use them as idea stimulators for your own original copy. Place an ad in one of the largest circulation publications you can find, then use the income from that ad to buy and place more advertising. In other words, use the money that comes in from the first ad to place similar ads in three or four other publications.

One of the inside secrets of the mail order business is in multiplying your advertising exposure. This means simply that you start with an ad in one publication, and from there, expand your exposure by advertising in more publications. Be patient, and wait for the returns from your current ads, then use that money to increase the number of people who will have a chance to see your ad. It's as simple as that, and it works every time. Try it and see for yourself.
All of this means that as you are getting started with a new mail order business, you have to reinvest all your business income back into the business. To do otherwise is a straight line to business failure.

How to Make $1,000 Profit with A 1,000 Name Mailing List!

If you've been in mail-order for a few years, or even a few months, you know how difficult it is to make a real profit. If you aren't careful, you'll lose money and be out of business very quickly. This report will help you make a real profit, and thereby stay in business. It reveals a simple, step-by-step plan for starting a money-making mail-order business by using direct mail. With this plan, you can make up to $1,000 profit for every 1,000 names that you mail to. That's $1,000 after paying all expenses! This plan was especially developed for use with direct mail, but you can also use these methods with inquiries that you receive from your ads.

Here is the plan...

1. Obtain a good mailing list -- preferably a proven list of buyers.

2. Mail an opportunity package to the people whose names are on the list, or to the people who answer your ads.

3. In your mailing package, include some good $1 offers. $1 isn't much these days, and many people will order several $1 items. We'll be conservative and assume you get orders that total $250. When you fill these orders, include other sales circulars. This will pull repeat sales that will increase your profit.

4. Include some good $2 offers. You could get 200 or more orders from every thousand that you mail. 200 at $2 is $400. When you fill these orders, include other sales circulars. This will get repeat sales.

5. Include some good $3 offers. You could get 100 or more $3 offers from every thousand that you mail. 100 times $3 is $300. When you fill these orders, be sure to include other sales circulars.
6. Include at least one good $5 offer. This could pull 50 or more orders from every thousand mailed. That's another $250, and this doesn't include repeat sales.

7. Include a good $10 offer. You can get 20 orders per 1,000. That's $200. Think about the profit you can make. From every 1,000 envelopes that you mail, you could get the following:

The Cell Block Presents TCB University

250 x $1 = $250
200 x $2 = $400
100 x $3 = $300
50 x $5 = $250
20 x $10 = $200

Add all this together, and that's $1,400! Now, deduct $400 to pay for postage, mailing lists, printing, plus expenses for filling orders and you have a profit of $1,000 or more for just a few hours of easy work. And this doesn't even include profits from repeat sales! With a well-designed package of offers, your repeat sales can pull in several thousand dollars from every 1,000 names!

Note: How much could you make if you get your postage stamps FREE? To learn, read my report "HOW TO GET FREE POSTAGE STAMPS!"

This step-by-step plan is based on mailing 1,000 envelopes, but you don't need to mail 1,000 all at once. Go slowly and constantly reinvest your profits. If you are a cautious type, start by mailing 50-100 per week. 100 a week is just 20 per day, Monday through Friday. You can get that many ready to mail while you watch TV! Clear off your coffee table or set up a folding card table. If necessary, use some cardboard boxes. Spread your circulars out in front of you, and then assemble them into 20 mailing packages. Address the envelopes, insert the circulars into the envelopes, seal the envelopes, place stamps on the envelopes. Now you're finished! That wasn't so hard, was it? The first two or three weeks may be a tad difficult, but after that, you should start getting orders. Then you'll know you're really making money and your work will be a lot easier. I guarantee it!

The "secret" that no one will tell you is this... Millions of people try to make money in mail order. Over 98% eventually fail. 90% fail in the first year. 75%. -- that's 3 out of every 4 -- quit within 3 months. Most of these people think that mail order is an easy way to get rich quick without working. When they learn the truth, they give up and start looking for another way to get rich. Now, a small number of dealers make a good living selling products to these wannabe millionaires. A few dealers even get rich. You can also become a wealthy dealer, but you will have to work. There aren't easy ways to get rich without working!!

How to Get Free Mailing Lists, Stamps & Envelopes!

If you intend to stay in the mail order business, you will have to learn how to get the right customers. It isn't difficult to locate the right buyers for the items you have to sell, but learning how can take many years of trial and error.

The best way to get orders is by the Direct Mail Method. This method is the most successful and the best used of all the option open to dealers. Direct Mail is simply described in most instruction manuals as the bulk of mail order in which various offers of various types are mailed directly to the names obtained from mailing list suppliers or names taken from phone books, etc. All these methods are fine, but you have to pay for the names. This, of course, cuts into your profits.

For years, I have gotten FREE names, FREE envelopes, and FREE postage stamps by using the BEST method ever created to get REAL buyers. How do I do this?

Some years ago, I placed a small classified ad in one of the best periodicals in the business. The ad offered FREE information about making money at home. The ad cost me very little and brought in several thousand replies. However, I didn't request any postage, which I should have done. Presently, I run an ad just like the one I ran a few years ago, but now I ask for a self-addressed, stamped envelope, or a SASE. My replies aren't as great as they were before, but I get plenty of FREE stamped envelopes.

If you have a good piece of information that can be cheaply printed on one side of an 8.5" x 11" sheet of paper, then you can offer this FREE as described in the outline above. When requests for the information pour in, stuff other information (fliers) into the envelope with the requested material. Most likely you will get several bites in addition to the other items you wished to sell. For example, let's say you sell books by mail, like I do. If you can offer a FREE catalog to inquirers, then you will get MORE than your fair share of replies.

In conclusion: Offering FREE INFORMATION is the BEST WAY to get FREE NAMES, STAMPS & ENVELOPES! Try it!

The Cell Block Presents TCB University

Customer Service Tips for Mail Order!

Can we be too good to our customers? No way! Our customers are the backbone of our business! They're right, no matter what! This may be, but I'm sorry to disagree with these sentiments. As small, honest, legitimate businesses, we have a tendency to place our product quality above money. While this is the "right" way of building a strong, solid business, there are nevertheless customers who will try to take advantage of you. You have to learn how to notice this possibility coming and "bow out gracefully" without losing the customer.

Remember that most newcomers to the world of mail order think that they are ordering from BIG companies just because we have a company name! They cannot conceive how poor and struggling a lot of us really are. They think we can absorb costs and because they are poor themselves, will often try to take advantage of people like us. (If they only realized the all-too-common situation of a mail order dealer going "in the hole" for bank charges on a $2 check that bounces...)

But because we are honest people who place our product ABOVE money we sometimes let people walk all over us. For example, one mail order dealer in shareware computer disks is normally so happy when an order comes in that he ends up giving the customer ten times what he paid for. He feels that he must go overboard to keep the customer happy.

Unfortunately, a lot of people will take advantage of a situation like this. They think, "Hey, if I can get this much for hardly anything, I'll see how much more they'll give me. Look at all the "freebies" I could get and all the money I can save." These customers will lose respect for you. This line of thinking, however, is only short term. Sure, as a customer you might get some more free stuff with the next order, but pretty soon the business owner will realize what's going on. Then you'll lose that business contact forever!

As a dealer, you can learn to give your customers what they pay for. Go that extra mile on special requests, but never over-extend yourself if it means lost profits to your business. This line of thinking will cause you to set yourself up to be taken advantage of and then you will become resentful toward your customers, which IS bad.

In mail order, we all have the ability to make ourselves look "richer" than we really are. We can work co-op deals with other people to barter and trade for things we don't have and could never pay for. Then, when orders are filled professionally, the customer suddenly thinks the mail order dealer has a lot of money to spread around and can afford to lose a few dollars on them.

If a customer does not send the correct amount for you to fill his or her order, simply write them a nice letter explaining that they did not enclose the proper amount. Send them an invoice showing the amount they still owe and bill them before filling the order.

If someone calls you with a good "pitch" to fill their order before they pay you, kindly explain your company policy is to receive payment first since they are a new customer. No other explanation is necessary.

However, don't go overboard, and end up looking "crazy". If a customer forgets to enclose a stamp for "details", go ahead and send him the information. It would be silly to spend another 49 cents just to tell them to send you the stamp... At least he's "in your store" and could end up sending you a large order.
Finally, some dealers refuse to take personal checks because they are afraid they might bounce. Again, this is not good customer service, since it can be a hassle for people to go out and buy a money order; most people do have checking accounts, and don't write bad checks. This kind of thinking could cost you lots of orders. Simply hold the order for at least two weeks, allowing time for the check to clear the bank. If it's bad, you'll know soon enough, and you can simply decline to fill the order. Use common sense, and you'll have many happy customers!

 ## The Big Money Secrets to Selling Books by Mail!!

Selling books by mail is one of the "ideal" spare-time business ventures that can be operated from your home, and with very minimal investment, can make you very rich! However, there's a lot you must learn about this kind of business; a lot to learn, a lot to understand, and a lot of common sense required.

The first thing you need to know is where to get the books -- the kinds of books -- that sell best via mail order. Selecting your source of supply, deciding which types of books you want to sell, and arranging a working relationship with these suppliers is your first step. Be sure you know which supplier has which books, the quantity discount prices, and the drop-ship requirements. It's best to set up a file on or for each of your suppliers; keep a copy of each of their latest catalogs, and some sort of record of all dealings you have with them.

Once you're organized with a source of supply, getting started is pretty easy. One way might be to acquire a series of money-making reports that range 2-3 pages in length, such as this one, that sell for a couple dollars each. Then, you run a classified ad in some of the national mail order publications reaching extra-income opportunity seekers.

Such an ad might read: FREE REPORT! $50,000 profit each year! Spare time, home-operated business. Send SASE for details: (Your name and address) Your secret to success in selling books by mail will lie in what you put into all those self-addressed, stamped envelopes you receive in response to your ad. Of course, the first thing you have to put in those envelopes is the "free report" you promised in your ad. We have a number of reports describing a plan that can make $50,000 a year for an energetic and determined extra-income opportunity seeker and have used all of them quite successfully in accordance with the plan we're describing to you here.

Now then, in addition to the "free report", as promised in your ad, and in order to sell books, you have to include what is known as your "follow-up" package. Doing this is quite simple and should almost be automatic. You'll need a full-page circular advertising one of the books you're selling. To see and understand this ingredient, collect the advertising sheets you receive from all the book clubs, relative to their "featured selection" circulars. Remember here that the more original and different than the "other" advertisers you can make your circulars, the more books you'll end up selling. Still, you may not want to undertake the work or have the extra finances to hire to have "feature selection" advertising circulars made up for you. In that case, simply take one of the full-page circulars advertising a particular book, sent out to you by one of your suppliers.

Following the successful methods used by all the Book-of-the-Month Clubs, in addition to your full-page circular advertising a specific book -- a featured selection -- you should include a sheet of other titles (alternate selection) for your customers to consider ordering.

We've found through many years of experience, that the best order-producing list of other availabilities to choose from is one of our lists of money-making reports. The psychology behind this is explained thusly: If your customer buys the "featured selection", he may not want to spend "another big chunk of money" right then on another book. However, since you would like him to spend more, you offer him a number of "inexpensive" reports that he can choose from, and, in the end, he'll probably spend more on the featured selection and several reports than he would have if he had purchased two books! Them, too, he might not want the featured selection, or he may already have it. In that case, you offer him the list of reports related to his interests, none of which will break his budget, and you've still made money/gotten an order from him! These are very important things to consider and think about every time you send out a mail order offer.

Generally, you do not need to include either a separate order form or a self-addressed envelope with your order-solicitation package. However, we would advise you to have your featured selection circular, and your alternate selection list printed on colored paper; say, your featured selection circular printed on white paper with red or blue ink, and your alternate selection printed on yellow or canary colored with black ink. This tends to give your mailing piece a bit of class, and at the same time tends to stimulate the prospects into buying more than just ordinary white paper with black ink. Give it some thought, try it, check your results and then decide from there.

I've just explained the "nitty gritty" of how to get organized, set yourself up in the book-selling business, and how to operate if profitably. But, unless you have everything pre-planned, your fledgling business may die before you've even scratched the surface of your potential profit picture.

It's necessary that you have a different "featured" selection circular and list of alternate selections to send out each time you send something out to your prospects or customers. Thus, before you begin, it will pay you to elect about 18 different books to call featured selections, or "Best Buy of the Month."
Make sure you have a full-page circular for each of these books -- have a supply of each of them printed and in stock -- then either number them or arrange them in the order you want to use them. You should have the same kind of supply and arrangement for your lists or alternate selections.

With books, it will be necessary to always be on the lookout for new books you can use as featured selections in your customer follow-up program. A supply of 18 will get you started, but as your business grows, you'll find some of your customers ordering every book you offer, and thus, in order to keep them buying from you, you'll have to keep offering new selections to them.
With your lists of alternative selections, this is not so important. Actually, you can start out with about 100 or so reports, and from this list, make up an alternative selection list of about 25 titles for each list. After you've gone through 100 of these reports -- 4 different alternative selection lists -- you can go back and mix the selections from each list -- 6 from list one, 6 from list two and so on.

It's important that you get your customer's order on its way just as quickly after receiving it as possible. When you're having, a supplier drop-ship for you, the best thing is to accumulate all your orders -- filling in your dropship order from each day's mail -- and then on Saturday of each week, writing your check to each supplier, enclosing the dropship order forms, sealing it and getting it in the mail. At the same time, you should send out your order acknowledgment notes and follow-up packages on the same day you receive them.

It may sound a little complicated, but it really isn't. And if you plan your business in detail before you place your first ad, have your follow-up materials printed in advance, and work this plan as we've explained it herein, you should have no trouble at all.

How to Start a Mail-Order Business on A Shoestring!

How can you start a mail-order business without spending a fortune? To start, the product that will sell the most, cost the least, and be free of trouble on shipping and all the other problems that "normal" mail-order products have, would obviously be the best.

Only if there were such a product, right?

Well, there is! And it is selling information by mail, whether it's books, booklets, tapes or reports. However, since we are discussing shoestring investment that eliminates, at least for now, books, tapes and booklets. What remains is selling reports by mail. Reports can be any typed information, but the best-selling information products, and the cheapest to reach customers, is selling one-page reports through low-cost ads.

The best way to start would seem to be to type up your own reports, but that means having a typewriter, and if you don't have one, the expense of getting one would violate our shoestring goal. But there is a cheaper way, however, and in some ways, it's even better: buy some reports that are already typed! You then would not need a typewriter, and the reports would still be very inexpensive. Most dealers who sell reports (with reprint rights!) charge no more than $1.00-$2.00 each. You may find some dealers who sell them cheaper, but they are usually not on 8.5 x 11 paper. You would have to get them retyped, and there goes our goal of doing all this on a shoestring. You want to make sure the reports you buy are on 8.5 x 11 paper, like the one you're reading now, so when you start selling them you can simply copy them on a low-cost copying machine as needed.

Being that you can copy your report(s) for around 10¢ each, then turn and sell them each for $1.00-$2.00, you can make a great profit. The biggest expense, however, that you will have, will be advertising, whether it's via classified ads, direct mail, or some other form you decide upon. You may have seen ads by mail order dealers or printers that will show you (for a price) how to get free advertising or almost free direct mailings, but you should always be cautious of these offers. It is much wiser to instead learn how to do it yourself so that you can keep accurate track of your numbers.

SUMMARY OF SELLING INFO BY MAIL ON A SHOESTRING...

Buy reports that come with reprint rights and that are printed on 8.5 x 11 paper. Buy several, until you find a few that you really like, and you know other will also like.

You must place TEST classified ads, in the proper types of publications, depending on the information you are selling, and keep track of which ones bring you the most responses.

How to Get Orders in Your Mailbox 365 Days A Year!

Don't you want to receive orders EVERY DAY OF THE YEAR? You can, if you have a post office box, and if you sell something that people want. I'll try and explain what people need so that you can profit from what I have learned over the years.
Most dealers believe a profit cannot be made unless items with big price tags are offered to the public. This is far from the truth. To keep the mail coming in on a regular basis, it is important to use "good will" and leader items. These are good-pulling offers that keep the dollars rolling in DAILY! In an average week, leader items selling for a couple of quarters or a dollar can bring dozens and dozens of orders. Offering valuable information, for example, with the price tags of .50 and $1.00 build customer interest and can create regular, repeat buyers.
For years, I have offered information for .50 and $1.00, and I find that these are not only big sellers, but they also build customer trust and a mailing list that I can use over and over again! Most of my "cheap" offers are short mini-folios

containing a few thousand helpful words. My cost is only a few pennies to print. My profit margin is not enormous, with the present cost of envelopes, printing and postage. But those who send me quarters and dollars usually return with larger orders. My repeat trade has always been above 50%. Selling information for a dollar or less may not seem very profitable to you, but getting the names of interested mail buyers is the name of the game!

Selling "Big Mail" is an excellent way to get names of mail buyers. After you get 100 orders, you can sell these names for up to $5.00 per 100. You can get enormous response to your ads if you just use your imagination. If you have a particular piece of information that hasn't made the rounds, put the material in your own words and sell it. One dealer sells the addresses of several companies that offer wholesale printing and his ad reads as follows: "Cheap Printing! List of 50 Discount Printers, $1.00!" This ad produces 20-30 orders EVERY DAY OF THE YEAR! That is more than $9,000 a year from one, small classified ad! You can easily duplicate this man's efforts! Simply sell a good piece of information and watch the dollars roll in every day! This is how you keep your mailbox full 365 days a year.

 ## Ad Designing Tips!

No matter if you are creating a tiny one-inch ad or an 11 x 17 newsletter, the design can have a huge effect on readability, understanding and effectiveness. Right off the bat, your ad needs the reader's eyes to follow and easily flow down the page from point to point. The whole idea here is to keep from building walls your reader has to climb over or around.

The words you use will keep the reader motivated to get your message. But if your design uses a wide variety of typefaces, different colors of type, sections in all caps, or pictures and graphics that force the reader's eye to jump around the page trying to follow you, few will make it to the finish line.

By carefully placing all the elements of your ad, you can allow a reader's eye to gracefully flow from your headline right down to your close. A letter ad is pretty easy. Just use a type size large enough to be easily read. Double space between paragraphs. More white space tends to make it easier to read.
A flyer may need the help of a picture or illustration. And a balanced design isn't necessarily the best for readability. More likely, putting the headline flush left or flush right, pictures or graphics on the other side of the page will add interest and

actuality make it easier to read.

Still, use lower case type even in headlines except for some special effect. And, please don't vary the type size or style randomly from line to line. It renders it nearly impossible to easily read.

When you have several pieces of art, you can direct the reader as to which one to look at first by making that one larger. Another way is to place the art one under the other, making it obvious what order they are to be in.

 ## Avoiding Mail Order Mistakes!

Not everyone has worked in an office atmosphere all his life. And when this type of person decides to go into a mail order business he doesn't know the first thing about communicating properly with other dealers and potential customers. This lack of communication can close a new mail order business faster than lightening.

Here are some tips to make your transition smoother.

Address your envelope properly. You should use a #10 business-size envelope, not the short ones you use to write to your mother. The envelope should contain the full name and address of the person you are writing as well as YOUR full name and address in the upper left-hand corner. If the letter is undeliverable because a dealer has closed his business, your will get the letter back if your return address is in the upper left-hand corner. In addition, if something should happen to the contents inside the envelope the dealer can contact you because of your return address.

Try to avoid handwriting your return address. Sometimes these are impossible to read. If you can't afford pre-printed envelopes by all means order some address labels for $1.25 per 1,000 from one of the several mail order firms advertising these things. Neon or glistening-type return labels are hard to read so try to avoid those too. Plain white ones with black ink will do fine.
Include a note or letter. Nothing is more frustrating than to receive an order from a customer with a check or cash enclosed with NO explanation of what the person is ordering. Beginners often forget that the average mail order dealer has hundreds, even thousands of products they offer. Many of those items might be priced the same. An example of a good cover letter would be:

Dear (fill in the name):

I noticed your ad in (name of publication) and would like to order your (name of product you are ordering). Thank you for your attention to this matter. (Your name and address)

You can write this information on a post-it notes and attach it to your check. However, it is more professional to use a standard sheet of 8 ½ X 11 paper and put your name and address at the top of the sheet. This way, if the envelope is non-readable or your return address is marked up in any way, the dealer can read your name and address and fill your order. In your cover letter, you might want to mention that you are new to mail order and would appreciate any information to help you out. Often, dealers extend a helpful hand to help others.

Don't expect your order in two days. Some people will see an advertisement or order an item on Monday and expect to receive it back by Thursday of the same week. This is usually impossible. It normally takes three days to receive first-class mail. It takes many dealers three to ten days to fill an order. Add another three days for delivery of the order to the customer, and a full two weeks could have elapsed between date of order and date of delivery.

Not everyone provides 24-hour service, especially in the mail order business. Most beginners don't realize that there are some mail order people processing an average of 200 to 1,000 pieces of mail per day. If you place an order with a national mail order house, don't they tell you to allow 4-6 weeks for your order to arrive? Give small dealers the same courtesy.

Having a mail order business is a lot of fun. It is exciting, and you get to meet a lot of great people. However, it is also a business and should be treated as such. If you are really serious and you have never had any office-related exposure, at least take an afternoon to read a book you can get free at the library on starting your small business. It will be worth your effort, and you can then start making friends and reaping the rewards of getting money in your mailbox on a daily basis.

 # How to Publish Your Own Ad Sheet for Big, BIG Profits!

Thousands of mail order ad sheets are published every month. Most of them are printed inexpensively by photocopy. Others incorporate reading material which increases their number of readers. Articles written on the subject of mail order are incentives for the readers to get more involved in the business of operating a home enterprise. Publishing the advertising messages of other individuals is a great responsibility. If one is not dependable or disciplined in carrying out the duties of publishing, then this business should NOT be attempted. The work involved can be as simple as you make it, or complicated. It cannot be put aside for a later date, as publishing means keeping a schedule, no matter how tired or involved in something else you may be.

Starting a publication is very simple and can be quite profitable. There are two routes to take in laying down the ground floor for a proposed publication: You must decide whether you want to set the ad copy on a typewriter or computer typesetter or accept only camera-ready ads from clients. Copy that is camera-ready is anything that is ready to be printed and needs no typesetting. The latter is best for new publishers as the only work involved is pasting up ads.

To get a new publication on the road to prospering, it is best to advertise the first issue at a discount rate. In other words, cover your printing cost, but keep your advertising rates low enough to obtain as many accounts as possible for the first issue or two. The following ad will bring in many advertising accounts to you:

"75 Cents Per Inch! Your 1" Camera-Ready Ad Printed and Mailed For Just 75. A 2" ad For Only $1.00!"

The above ad should be placed in several publications to ensure a good number of incoming orders. Your next step is to give your publication a good name. The easy method is to look through a magazine or newspaper and clip out an eye-catching heading such as: BARGAIN SALE, DISCOUNT DAYS, or anything else you feel is a suitable name for your publication (also known as masthead or logo).

The most difficult part of your work will be the paste-up. This can be easily figured out by looking at other ads sheets you have received in the mail. Remember to use a light blue or yellow pencil to draw lines and margins on paper, as these do not photograph, while pencil does.

Accept ads on white or yellow paper only, printed in black or red ink. Colored papers will come out as a blotch when printed unless the printer has the facilities to filter out color from individually colored ad copy. Always use rubber cement to do your paste-up and a cement eraser to remove globs of glue that remain after you do the layout.

The Cell Block Presents TCB University

If you follow the brief outline I have given you, you should be making a nice income very shortly. Many small publishers earn from $5,000 to $10,000 yearly printing only one ad sheet on small paper.

GET MONEY: Self-Educate, Get Rich & Enjoy Life, Vol. 1

Part Three: Surviving Prison

The Cell Block Presents TCB University

Paroling from Prison (my 2 cents)

If this topic applies to you, you are extremely fortunate; it means that you will have a second chance at life, which is obviously a beautiful thing. Keep in mind that there are many prisoners this topic does not apply to....

I cannot say that I am an expert on paroling from prison, as I have never paroled. Furthermore, I do not go out of my way to research things relevant to paroling, as I have life in prison without the possibility of parole.

However, while I am not an expert on the topic of parole, I am a man with 2 eyes, a brain (that is not on drugs), and awareness, and I cannot help but see prisoners parole and often come right back. Personally, I find watching prisoners parole & return over and over again to be absolutely disgusting. It means they have not learned that prison is a terrible place to be & there is a lot more to life than this bullshit lifestyle, and that they are still taking their freedom/life for granted & not respecting/appreciating the blessing of another chance – something that lot of us are only left to fantasize about....

Now, while I cannot give you information from a perspective of a man who has paroled or is paroling, I can tell you what I do know – what I've learned from watching people leave & come back over & over again, & what my common sense tells me – in hopes that it helps you not come back; if for nothing else, so that you do not disgust me.

Planning & preparation:

From the minute, you get to prison you should start preparing for your parole. For you, prison is not your life; it is merely an experience that will someday end. And when that day comes, you should be fully prepared.

What I mean by preparing for your parole is; making the necessary changes & learning the necessary information that will ensure you don't only get out, but stay out.

2 questions you need to ask-yourself/answer:

The first thing you need to do is ask yourself & answer 2 very important questions: 1) how can I make it out of prison as soon as possible? 2) What do I need to do while I'm in prison to prepare myself for success when I get out so that I never return?

Priority # 1:

Whatever answer you come up with for question #1 should be your primary focus; your main objective should be to make that date. Regardless of how you play the game or what image you try to promote; your focus needs to stay aimed at your date & what you need to do to get out of prison as soon as possible that should always remain priority #1.

Strategizing:

Create & customize a plan/strategy that will allow you to reach your objective/priority #1. Keep in mind that your blessing required you to figure out a different strategy than a prisoner who will not parole; you have your opportunity of paroling to lose while a prisoner who will never parole doesn't even have to factor that into his decision-making.

For example, I have life without the possibility of parole plus two 25-to-life sentences, & since I've been in prison I've caught 2 DA referrals. However, none of them have been picked up – including one for an "attempted murder" that was caught on camera & where the victim snitched & said it was me.

The reason it was not picked up, though, is because I have too much time; it's not worth the money the state would have to spend to try the case. But for someone who has a date, the DA may pick up something as minor as getting caught with a $50 paper of heroin or a razor blade.

So, while I can sell drugs on the yard all day long or stab people who offend me (because I don't have the possibility of paroling anyway), if you do have the blessing of a second chance, then by all means necessary you need to stay away from problems or trouble of any kind – you should do your absolute best to remain discipline free; you should not risk doing anything that will keep you in prison for even one extra day.

Only you can decide what's best for you, & you obviously need to remain safe. (The overall priority #1), but throughout this book I explain several options for dealing with situations, & I suggest you pay close attention to the ones that are more suitable for your reality versus the ones more suitable for mine. Even if you're in a position to where you must "play the game," you can still move very carefully & slick – like Shorty, in chapter.

Proof of Accomplishments:

It would also be a good idea to take into consideration what you are in prison for, & if you have to impress the parole board or not in order to get out. If you do, I suggest you earn as many certificates as possible. For example, if drugs were involved in your case, it might be wise to take a drug class or 2 where you will earn a certificate you can take to board with you. Or if you have some kind of assault case, an anger management certificate might look good on your behalf.

In any case, if you will be going before the parole board, it's probably wisest to get as many (any and all) certificates as you can – parenting, anger management, drugs/alcoholics anonymous, trades, correspondence courses, etc. Doing so will allow you to show the board what you've learned – something more valuable than you just telling them.

Learn what's worked for others in your situation:

It's always a good idea to study & learn what has worked for those who've succeeded at what you're trying to do, & making parole is just what Gerald T. Balone has done.

Gerald, a man who had a 50 – year – to – life sentence, was released in 2007 after surviving 37 ½ years. He has since written a book titled, "A Former Insider's Guide to Parole: A Manual for Anyone Trying to Get out of Prison," in which he explains how he was successful at making parole after so many years.

Gerald sells his book for $20.00, & it can be ordered on his website GTBSpeaks.com; where you can also read book reviews, as well as the table of contents. Or, if you don't have internet access, it can also be ordered by sending a facility check or money order to:

GTB Speaks, LLC
Attn: Book Order
1200 William Street, PO Box 686
Buffalo, NY 14240-0686

Priority #2 (Prepare for it now):

Once you've figured out what you're going to do in order to get out of prison, you need to figure out what you should be doing now to prepare for when you do get out, so that you can be successful & remain out.

Two questions you need to ask-yourself/answer:

From my experience, the majority of prisoners who parole come back for 2 major reasons: 1) they are unable to find work & make money/a-living legally. 2) They are forced to parole right back to the environment they came from, & they get caught back up in the same lifestyle – drugs, crime, & all-around negativity.

With that said, here are 2 very important questions that you need to ask yourself & find answers for: 1) What do I need to do now to ensure I have the ability to make money/a-living legally when I get out? 2) When I get out, how can I avoid from getting sucked right back into the environment/lifestyle I came from?

Strategizing – work/money:

When strategizing how you are going to be financially successful when you get out, figure out what it is you want to do as a job/career, & what you need to study/learn in order to prepare yourself for that job/career.

For example, would it be beneficial for you to take correspondence courses & earn a degree or 2, or would it be best for you to read specific books that specialize in your area(s) of interest? These are all things you should figure out early on in your prison stay & start working towards as soon as possible.

Whatever you do, even if you already have "connections" for work on the outside, never rely solely on that. Don't use that to just sit around & be lazy in prison. For 1) just sitting around would be a waste of very valuable time and for 2) you should never rely on anything or anyone other than, yourself. I don't care if your wife's brother has a friend whose dad's cousin owns his own construction company & will hook you up when you get out. If that's the case & it works out for you, great; but hardly rely on it. It is much wiser to rely on what you have & what you can do.

For more information & ideas in regard to this point, read/re-read chapter "use your time wisely." If you use your time wisely, all of this will already be included in your game plan.

Strategizing – around your old environment/life-style:

Coming up with a strategy to avoid your old environment can be a bit difficult – for several reasons. For 1) parole will probably force you to parole to the county you caught your case in. For 2) most of your resources – wife, family, friends, etc. – probably live in the same exact place/neighborhood they did before you came to prison. And for 3) sometimes they – your "resources" – are actually the same people you should be trying to avoid.

It is possible to get your parole transferred to another county/state if you have some kind of positive support there & can convince your parole agent to allow it. And, if you're open to it, transitional housing (halfway – home – type – programs) is always an option. These are things you will have to work on with your parole officer, should you decide they are in your best interest.

If you feel you really have little choice but to parole fight back to the environment – people, place, & things – that cultivated/influenced you to get caught up in the things that led you to prison in the first place, it might be more difficult to succeed with the various influences & temptations you are sure to be surrounded by, but it is definitely not impossible. I am certain that with enough dedication & determination, anything – and this includes remaining free – can be done.

In any case, while you do your time in prison, I suggest you to some heavy soul searching; get to know who you truly are, who you want to be, & decide if living your life in prison is really the way you want to like. Because in the end, what it all boils down to is that, it is you who will make your decisions.

 Mental Health: The Secrets

Not only is it important that you stay physically healthy in order to survive prison, but it is as equally important that you stay mentally healthy. The prison experience/environment can easily take its toll on the minds of its men, so if you wish to survive, you must learn to overcome the challenges you are sure to face. No matter how strong your body is, prison will eat you alive if your mind is weak.

Despite what people on the outside may or may not think, it is important for you to understand that prisons are designed to mentally break its prisoners (you!) down. Once a man is broken down mentally, he starts to break spiritually. And one he's spiritually broken, he's as good as dead....

Furthermore, a mentally broken man is easier to control, as being mentally broken is to be tired. When he is tired, it's harder for him to fight. When it's harder for him to fight, it's easier for "them" to win. It is obviously to "their" benefit that you are weak; therefore, "they" have intentionally designed "their" system to exhaust you, and it is up to you to fight against falling a victim to that. In addition to the above, your psychological battle is not only with the depressing predicament that you find yourself in or the mental roller coaster designed by prison to suck out your energy and steal your spirit, but with your fellow prisoners, as well. Prison is a bloody shark tank full of great whites, and your fellow prisoners wish to suppress you just as much as anyone else. As explained in the mental warfare section of this book, you must learn to spot mental attacks from your fellow prisoners as well as defend yourself from them; and, just as importantly, you must also learn to spot and defend yourself from the mental attacks/wars waged against you by prison itself.

Here are my tips to staying mentally healthy and strong while you are in prison.

Keep your cell light on:

For some reason, many prisoners like to keep their cell light off so that their cell remains dark all day. Why someone would want to live in the dark is beyond me, but it is an extremely common thing to do in prison.

Don't fall into this kind of program. Instead, keep your light on and live. Look at it like this: Light is life, and dark is death. When my celly wants to keep the light off all day I can physically feel a difference in my body. Too much darkness will bring upon depression. We are like plants: put us in sunlight, we will grow and live; put us in the dark, we will wither and die.

Don't sleep too much:

Another thing a lot of prisoners like to do is sleep all day. However, it's a mistake; don't do it. Sleeping too much will not only make you always feel sluggish and sleepy, but it, too, will bring upon depression.

Exercise:

Make sure you physically exercise at least a little bit each day. You have to keep yourself active. If you let a car sit too long without starting it, driving it around, etc., it's not going to run right. Well, the same thing goes for your body. A healthy body will help you keep a healthy mind, exercising will help you release tension and stress.

Don't dwell:

I know life isn't necessarily going your way right now. However, don't sit around and dwell on your situation all day. It won't change anything, it will only add to your misery.

Instead of dwelling, turn whatever injustice has been done to you into a reason to fight. Rather than dwell or get depressed, get angry and channel that energy into something positive and/or beneficial; let your situation fuel your fire. Rather than dwelling on your situation, change it.

Stay positive:

Despite your situation, you must remain positive. Too much negativity will kill you. Positivity (+) will add to your life; negativity (-) will take it away....

In addition to that, avoid negative people. They are like "energy vampires"; they will suck all the positive energy right out of you with their constant pessimism.

Have a sense of humor:

It's important and healthy to have a good sense of humor. No matter what your situation is, always try to look for the humor in things. Laughter heals.

Have a Focus:

Set goals for yourself and focus on them. Whether it's writing a book, studying something you're passionate about, or getting into something else that's time-consuming, escape prison by finding something positive and beneficial to do and focus on it. When you are focused on something, you will be too busy to dwell, stress, feel sorry for yourself, etc.

Read inspirational stories:

Another thing I think is a good idea is to read inspirational stories. Whether you're religious or not, I find that "Guideposts" (magazines) have a lot of stories that give me a good feeling each time I read them. The "Chicken Soup for the Soul" is a good series too. And they even have a "Chicken Soup for the Prisoner's Soul."

Taking in good, positive, inspirational information is healthy. Whether it's reading books with these kinds of stories, or even watching TV shows like "Secret Millionaire" or "Home Makeover," intake as much positive and healthy information as you can.

Keep the faith; remain hopeful:
Despite what your reality is today, you must remain hopeful. You'd be amazed how far faith and hope will take you. You must never give up. As long as you remain hopeful and continue to fight, you will have a chance of succeeding. If you lose hope and stop fighting, you will for sure not have a chance of succeeding. It's kind of like the concept, "you can't win if you don't play."

Religion:

I cannot say that I am a real religious man. However, as I get older, I have a much clearer understanding of the essence and concept of religion. It now makes sense to me why people find so much strength in religion, and it all comes down to keeping faith and remaining hopeful.

If you have a religion, practice it. Religion is a positive intake. Therefore, it will help you stay on a positive path and remain faithful.

Mental relaxation:

Finding time to relax your mind is crucial. You should dedicate at least 15 minutes a day to practicing some kind of relaxation technique – meditation, etc. In prison's chaotic environment, it is very important that you maintain peace of mind.

Note: I find calmative breathing to be a great, simply way to reduce anxiety, and it can be done anywhere, anytime. All you have to do is inhale through your nose, hold it for a count of four, and exhale slowly through pursed lips until you have expelled all of the air in your lungs. Try it; you will immediately feel more relaxed.

Surviving the Hole: The Secrets

Let me begin by explaining the following…

The hole is technically an informal name given to units where prisoners are locked down and usually in some form of isolation. Other informal names you may hear are solitary confinement, lock-up units, or lockdown units. The formal name may differ depending on what state you're in but the most common name is "Administrative Segregation" (Ad-Seg). Prisoners are sent to the hole (Ad-Seg) for disciplinary, security, or safety purposes.

SHU stands for "Security Housing Unit." And while the hole is often a temporary placement, if one is found guilty of a SHUable rule violation or deemed a security threat to the general population – maybe because he has been validated as an associate or member of a prison gang and is said to have a high influence among other prisoners – one will be sent to the SHU. Other names you might hear of SHU-type facilities are "management unit" or "control unit." However, program and concept-wise, all lock-up units are similar in nature.

A bit of perspective:

When you're in prison, going to the hole is kind of like going to the county jail; whereas going to the SHU would be like going to prison. What I mean by that is, when you are free, on the streets, and you are accused or suspected of a crime, you are sent to the county jail while you fight your case. If you are convicted and the crime carries prison time, you will then be sent to prison. Well, when you're in prison, on a general population yard, that is prison's equivalence to being free. However, if you are accused or suspected of a "crime" (rule violation) while in prison, the Correctional Officers will arrest you and lock you up in the hole – where you will lose most of your privileges/freedom – while you wait to have your crime (rule violation) heard by a judge (Senior Hearing Officer). If you are convicted (found guilty) and the crime (rule violation) is SHUable, you will go to the SHU.

However, for the purpose of this chapter, I am going to use the common, generic name "the hole" to refer to any unit with a lockdown/isolation concept.

The concept:

Prison's concept, in general, is to punish its prisoners by depriving them of freedom. The hole, however, takes punishment to another level, as its concept is sensory deprivation – to deprive prisoners of their five basic senses: sight, sound, smell, touch and taste. The idea of prison's administration is that, if they cannot break of control you by prison alone, where all of your rights as a free human being are stripped from you, they will break and control you by putting you in the hole, often for long periods of time, and strip you of all basic human senses. However, whether they are successful or not is often up to you....

How/why does this pertain to you?

Well, if you are doing a stretch in prison, odds are you will at some time end up in the hole for one reason or another. After all, it's not very difficult to find yourself in the hole, as some prisons will send you there for something as simple as a fistfight, which, in some prisons are a daily occurrence.

The experience:

While in the hole, with the exception of three showers and a few hours of yard a week (in most places), you will spend all your time locked down in your cell. You will have little or no contact with other prisoners – with the exception of your celly, if you have one, as some holes are single cell – and you will also have very little or no contact with the outside world, as prisoners in the hole are typically not allowed to use the phone, and only allowed two 1-hour, no-contact visits per week.

You will also have very little property – even less than the already little amount you are allowed in general population. Regardless of your reason for being in the hole, whether you killed somebody on the yard, you're under investigation for selling drugs, or you're there because you feel your life is in danger and you've requested protection, all prisoners are treated the same.

Personally, I don't necessarily mind being in the hole. I would rather be in general population because I have more access to things and can maintain my relationships better with people on the outside, as I have access to contact visits and phone calls; however, I have done a lot of time in the hole (SHU, Ad-Seg, etc.), so I have learned how to take advantage of the situation. Being in the hole allows me to escape the daily distractions that occur in the general population and focus on my work, which is what I like to do anyway. In fact, while I write/work-on this very chapter of "Surviving Prison," I am actually in CCI SHU, in Tehachapi, CA.

However, not everybody is able to survive the hole as well as others. The lack of human interaction (except for one's celly, if he has one, which can actually become a problem because of too much time together); the lack of contact with family and friends on the outside (which often leads to a loss of relationships); the feeling of being trapped in a cell for most of every day; the sometimes dead quietness, yet sometimes loud chaoticness; the constant hunger; the strip searches that take place every time one comes out the cell; etc., is often just too much for even a strong man to handle. Such a situation often leads to frustration, depression, and hopelessness.

If you find yourself in this situation there are things you can do to help yourself cope a little easier. In concept, this entire book will help you survive your time in the hole, but you should "up" the concepts to a more intense level, as doing time in the hole is much more intense (especially mentally) than doing time in the general population. In order to maintain your composure, you must learn to exercise extreme discipline and you must learn to survive on even less than you do in general population, oftentimes in even animal-like conditions.

Here are some things that I incorporate into my strategy when doing time in the hole, and I suggest you try to incorporate them into your strategy as well. You will notice that many of my suggestions appear elsewhere in this book, but for the specific purpose of surviving the hole I have listed them here for you...

Use your time wisely:

It is very important that you take advantage of your time in the hole, and, like in any situation, turn what is perceived as a negative into a positive. Don't just go to the hole and sleep. Instead, set goals for yourself, come up with a plan, and execute it. While in the hole is a perfect time to focus on your legal case, the book you've wanted to write, or study the subject(s) you've wanted to learn about. You are going to have a lot of time on your hands. However, time is valuable; use yours wisely and you will prosper.

Stay busy:

You are only using your time wisely if you are constantly busy. You should have no time to just sit around aimlessly. You will notice that a lot of prisoners who break under the pressure of being in the hole are the same ones who just lay around and/or talk out of their doors and/or in their vents all day. They are ambitionless and do nothing but sulk in their reality, allowing it to eat away at their sanity. Staying busy will help you mentally escape your environment, which is key to surviving one as hellish as the hole.

Reflect; organize your thoughts:

Use this down-time to get your thoughts in order. Reflect on the situation(s) that lead up to you being placed in the hole, what you may have done wrong, and how you can improve your strategy upon being released (if you're lucky enough to be released).

Furthermore, you should also use this time to reflect on your life as a whole, and how you can improve yourself from this point forward. Look deep into who you are as a man, decide exactly who and what it is you want to be, and how you can become the best you.

Correspond/Communicate:

If you were never into letter writing before, I suggest you learn to get in to it now, because it is extremely important to have regular correspondence with your family and friends on the outside. You being in prison is hard on your relationships, but you being in the hole is much, much harder. You must do all you can to maintain your relationships on the outside.

Furthermore, maintaining contact, communication, and support from your family and friends is extremely important in regard to your survival. Such correspondence will provide you with hope, and hope will help you push forward. I suggest that you also use this time to reach out and try to connect with other forms of outside support such as pen pals, network organizations, etc., so that you are in as much contact as possible with people in the free world.
Note: If you plan on doing something that you know is going to land you in the hole, I suggest you mini-write all your addresses and kiester them – wrap them in plastic and stick them up your asshole. You want to make sure that you can always maintain contact/communication with your people/resources.

Express yourself:

Being in isolation can limit the ways you are able to express yourself – both emotionally and creatively – but it still can and should be done. Keeping a written journal about your experience, writing down your personal ideas/philosophies, writing poetry and/or song lyrics is a good way to express yourself emotionally. Writing things such as magazine articles, plays, short stories and/or books is a great way to express yourself creatively; as is drawing.

Create a way to express yourself both emotionally and creatively. Doing so will help you release built-up emotion as well as give you something to focus on. Use your imagination and creativity to escape the boundaries of your cell's four walls.

Read:

Read as much as you can while in the hole. Reading will not only provide you with great knowledge, but also take you to another place mentally.

I suggest that you read books that are educational and relevant to your studies, but I also suggest that you read newspapers and magazines that will keep you up-to-date with news and interests that you have in the free world. You must never accept nor get used to prison. Keeping a piece of your thoughts focused on the free world will help you do so, as it will remind you that something much greater than your immediate environment exists.

Exercise:

Being cramped in a cell all day is unhealthy, so it is very important that you exercise regularly. Develop an exercise program and follow it. Try to stretch and use your muscles, as close to as much as you would if you were not in the hole.

Furthermore, exercising provides a way for you to release unwanted energy and stress. Not only is exercising good for your body physically, but mentally, too. While exercising is a great time to block out your environment, get your thoughts in order, and even meditate.

Lastly, even though you will have very little or no contact with other prisoners, you must keep yourself combat-ready at all times. You never know when your door will "accidently" open along with the door of a prisoner with whom you are at war with. Believe me, it happens; always be prepared for it.

Meditate:

It is very, very important that you take time out of each day – at least 15-30 minutes – to meditate. Meditating will allow you to release a lot of physical and mental stress. Study various meditation techniques and use the ones you feel work the best for you.

The Cell Block Presents TCB University

Mike Enemigo is a self-made, affluent "prisonpreneur" who turned his dirty hustle clean. He is the founder and executive publisher of The Cell Block – a company that publishes only works created in a prison cell. So far, he's published 15 books and has many more on the way.

GET MONEY: Self-Educate, Get Rich & Enjoy Life, Vol. 1

The Cell Block Presents TCB University

The Cell Block Presents TCB University

NEW NOW AVAILABLE IN BOOK FORMAT

Get Money
Self-Educate, Get Rich & Enjoy Life
3 Volume Series

Categories In Every Volume
- ✓ GET MONEY
- ✓ MAILBOX MONEY
- ✓ SURVIVING PRISON

Sections In Every Volume Filled With
- ✓ ALL NEW
- ✓ UP-TO-DATE
- ✓ IDEAS
- ✓ INSTRUCTIONS

ON HOW TO GET MONEY!

Each Book: Softcover, 6"x9", 125+ pages, B&W

Over $70 Worth of Reports in Each Volume

These books are part of a three volume series that provide educational information to prisoners, street hustlers and anyone who wants to learn how to get money and win legally in their quest for wealth and prosperity. Each volume has three sections Get Money, Mailbox Money & How to Survive Prison. Every section is filled with new, up to date ideas and instructions on how to get money.

ORDER SEPARATELY or ORDER ALL 3 - SAVE

☐ GET MONEY: Self-Educate, Get Rich & Enjoy Life, Vol. 1... $15.99 plus $5 s/h
☐ GET MONEY: Self-Educate, Get Rich & Enjoy Life, Vol. 2... $15.99 plus $5 s/h
☐ GET MONEY: Self-Educate, Get Rich & Enjoy Life, Vol. 3... $15.99 plus $5 s/h
☐ VALUE PAK: 3 BOOK SET, GET MONEY: Vol. 1, 2 &3... $39.99 plus $7 s/h

WE ACCEPT ALL CHECKS & MONEY ORDERS Payable to: **The Cell Block**

FREEBIRD PUBLISHERS, BOX 541, NORTH DIGHTON, MA 02764

AVAILABLE Amazon & FreebirdPublishers.com & TheCellBlock.net

WE NEED YOUR REVIEWS

Rate Us & Win!

We do monthly drawings for a FREE copy of one of our publications. Just have your loved one rate any Freebird Publishers book on Amazon and then send us a quick e-mail with your name, inmate number, and institution address and you could win a FREE book.

FREEBIRD PUBLISHERS
Box 541
North Dighton, MA 02764

www.freebirdpublishers.com
Diane@FreebirdPublishers.com

The Cell Block Presents TCB University

Thanks for your interest in Freebird Publishers!

We value our customers and would love to hear from you! Reviews are an important part in bringing you quality publications. We love hearing from our readers-rather it's good or bad (though we strive for the best)!

If you could take the time to review/rate any publication you've purchased with Freebird Publishers we would appreciate it!

If your loved one uses Amazon, have them post your review on the books you've read. This will help us tremendously, in providing future publications that are even more useful to our readers and growing our business.

Amazon works off of a 5 star rating system. When having your loved one rate us be sure to give them your chosen star number as well as a written review. Though written reviews aren't required, we truly appreciate hearing from you.

☆☆☆☆☆ **Everything a prisoner needs is available in this book.**
January 30, 201 June 7, 2018
Format: Paperback

A necessary reference book for anyone in prison today. This book has everything an inmate needs to keep in touch with the outside world on their own from inside their prison cell. Inmate Shopper's business directory provides complete contact information on hundreds of resources for inmate services and rates the companies listed too! The book has even more to offer, contains numerous sections that have everything from educational, criminal justice, reentry, LGBT, entertainment, sports schedules and more. The best thing is each issue has all new content and updates to keep the inmate informed on todays changes. We recommend everybody that knows anyone in prison to send them a copy, they will thank you.

* No purchase neccessary. Reviews are not required for drawing entry. Void where prohibited.
Contest date runs July 1 - June 30, 2019.

GET MONEY: Self-Educate, Get Rich & Enjoy Life, Vol. 1

INMATE SHOPPER, Book of Resources for Inmate Services   -2018-19 NEW ISSUE-
1000+ Listings AMERICA'S LARGEST Resources for Inmate Services. Everything you need from the outside while in prison is available in this ANNUAL ISSUE 2018-19, Split Year, June to June. All new content in each issue, constantly updated with products, services, resources, news, sport schedules, sexy non nude photo spread, pen pal section & more. Softcover, 8x10", B&W, 360+ pages... $26.99 ($19.99 plus $7 s/h)

SEXY GIRL PARADE, Non Nude Photo Book
Full color gloss non nude photos. A different photo on every page. Over $100 worth of sexy photos in one book, for one low price. Non nude prison friendly. Softcover, 8.3x6", GLOSS COLOR, 128 pages... $31.99 ($24.99 plus $7 s/h)

PEN PAL SUCCESS: The Ultimate Guide To Getting and Keeping Pen Pals
You've heard it said "The game is to be sold not told." Well, now a new book is doing all the telling about the game. In 20 information-dense chapters you'll DISCOVER the secrets. Pen Pal Success contains "insiders" wisdom especially for prisoners. You owe it to yourself to invest in this book! Softcover, 8x10", B&W, 225+ pages... $29.99 ($22.99 plus $7 s/h)

CELLPRENEUR: The Millionaire Prisoner's
Wish you could start a legitimate business from your cell? And not violate your prison rules? Do you have an idea that you wish you could license to another company and make money from it? They tell you "You can't start a business while in prison." Well the author did and book contains "insider's" wisdom especially for prisoners. You owe it to yourself to invest in this book! Softcover, 8x10", B&W, 250+ pages $29.99 (22.99 plus 7. s/h)

THE BEST 500+ NON PROFIT ORGS FOR PRISONERS and Their Families   -NEW 5th Ed.-
America's only up to date & comprehensive print resource of non profit orgs specifically for prisoners. Over 500+ Listings. All entries updated and new sections, Registry of Motor Vehicles by state, Social Security by state, Internal Revenue Service by state and region, Immigration by state and U.S. Congress by state and district. Softcover, 8x10", B&W, 160+ pages... $21.99 ($16.99 plus $5 s/h)

THE CELL CHEF Cook Book
The Cell Chef Cookbook is filled with hundreds of fantastic recipes, that can be simply made with everyday, commonly sold commissary/store foods. Every recipe has been tried and thoroughly tested. Loved by everyone. In the Cell Chef Cookbook the recipes are divided into four sections: Meals and Snacks, Sauces, Sandwich Spreads, Salsa and Dips, Drinks & Sweet Desserts. Softcover, Square 8.25X8.25"", B&W, 183 pages... $18.99 ($13.99 plus $5 s/h)

A YEAR OF THE CORCORAN SUN Book
This book filled with twelve issues of prison yard monthly newsletters compiled for hours of reading enjoyment. The book is packed full with news, entertainment, writing tips, publishing leads, resources, art, poetry, drama, and fiction by and for inmates and their loved ones. Softcover, 8x10", B&W, 240+ pages... $21.99 ($15.99 plus $6 s/h)

NO ORDER FORM NEEDED CLEARLY WRITE ON PAPER & SEND PAYMENT TO:
Freebird Publishers Box 541, North Dighton, MA 02764
DIANE@FREEBIRDPUBLISHERS.COM WWW.FREEBIRDPUBLISHERS.COM

The Cell Block Presents TCB University

ALL PRICES INCLUDE SHIPPING & HANDLING with TRACKING

LIFE WITH A RECORD: Reenter Society, Finish Supervision and Live Successfully
Information in this book help make sense of the major challenges facing ex-offenders today. Ten hard hitting chapters outline the purpose of making a Strategic Reentry it packs an amazing amount of material into its pages and gives you a quick, easy to follow, full spectrum of instruction. explores the most commonly confronted issues and attitudes that sabotage reentry. Addressing the whole reentry process. Softcover, 8x10", B&W, 360 pages $32.99 (25.99 plus $7 s/h)

KITTY KAT, Adult Entertainment Non Nude Resource Book
This book is jam packed with hundreds of sexy non nude photos including photo spreads. The book contains the complete info on sexy photo-sellers, hot magazines, page turning bookstore, sections on strip clubs, porn stars, alluring models, thought provoking stories and must see movies. Softcover, 8x10", Color covers, B&W interior, 185+ pages $31.99 ($24.99 plus $7 s/h)

HOT GIRL SAFARI, Non Nude Photo Book
Full color gloss non nude photos. A different photo on every page. Over $100 worth of sexy photos in one book, for one low price. Non nude prison friendly. Softcover, 8.3x6", GLOSS COLOR, 128 pages... $31.99 ($24.99 plus $7 s/h)

POST-CONVICTION RELIEF: Secrets Exposed
This book is full of information about how to get out of prison early. Cover to cover filled with motions and secrets used by real Habeas Corpus practitioners getting real results. This book will show you the simple way to: Get your case file; Analyze your case; Keep your records efficiently; Investigate your case, see what you deserve; Write simple effective motions; Get out of prison; EARLY!! Softcover, 8x10", B&W, 190+ pages $26.99 (19.99 plus 7. s/h)

S.T.O.P. Start Thinking Outside Prison
Thinking is very critical to one's success, failure, and survival. Every decision requires thinking. If not, many actions will be done on impulse. And impulsive behavior tends to bring about situations from which one needs to be rescued. S.T.O.P. was written as a movement to help promote a greater thinking process - a thinking process believed to slow down the recidivism rate within our communities. Softcover, 6x9", B&W, 70 pages $18.99 ($13.99 plus $5 s/h)

SOFT SHOTS, Non Nude Photo Book
Come see our beautiful ladies dressed in the tiniest of outfits and posing in many different alluring positions. Full color gloss non nude photos. A different photo on every page. Over $100+ worth of sexy photos in one book, for one low price. Non nude prison friendly. Softcover, 8.25x5.25", GLOSS COLOR, 150 pages... $31.99 ($24.99 plus $7 s/h)

GIFT Look Book 2018-19 Plus FREE SWAROVSKI Crystal Jewelry Book   -NEW BOOK-
With Every Book Receive a $15.00 Voucher We carry hundreds of high quality gifts for every occasion to fit every budget. Our gifts are made in America! Gift Baskets, Flowers, Chocolates & Candies, Personalized Gifts and more. We offer a complete line of custom gift baskets. Our flowers are delivered fresh in bud-form to open up full bloom in front of your loved ones. Our chocolates fresh made of the finest quality. Animated singing plush gifts. Softcover, 8x10", FULL COLOR, 110 pages $15.00 (Free s/h) **2 Books for $15, Free s/h Plus Credit Voucher**

NO ORDER FORM NEEDED CLEARLY WRITE ON PAPER & SEND PAYMENT TO:
Freebird Publishers Box 541, North Dighton, MA 02764
DIANE@FREEBIRDPUBLISHERS.COM WWW.FREEBIRDPUBLISHERS.COM

CPSIA information can be obtained
at www.ICGtesting.com
Printed in the USA
LVHW082240291120
672957LV00052B/998